15-MINUTE
FRENCH
LEARN IN JUST 12 WEEKS

Caroline Lemoine

Penguin Random House

REVISED EDITION
DK LONDON
Senior Editor Ankita Awasthi Tröger
Senior Art Editor Clare Shedden
Managing Editor Carine Tracanelli
Managing Art Editor Anna Hall
US Editor Heather Wilcox
US Executive Editor Lori Hand
Senior Production Editor Andy Hilliard
Senior Production Controller Poppy David
Jacket Design Development Manager Sophia MTT
Associate Publishing Director Liz Wheeler
Art Director Karen Self
Publishing Director Jonathan Metcalf

DK DELHI
Senior Editors Tina Jindal, Janashree Singha
Project Art Editor Anukriti Arora
Assistant Art Editor Sulagna Das
Managing Editor Soma B. Chowdhury
Senior Managing Art Editor Arunesh Talapatra
Senior Jacket Designer Suhita Dharamjit
Senior Jackets Coordinator Priyanka Sharma-Saddi
DTP Coordinator Pushpak Tyagi
DTP Designers Rakesh Kumar, Mrinmoy Mazumdar,
Manish Upreti
Hi-Res Coordinators Neeraj Bhatia, Jagtar Singh
Production Editor Vishal Bhatia
Production Manager Pankaj Sharma
Pre-production Manager Balwant Singh
Senior Picture Researcher Sumedha Chopra
Picture Research Manager Taiyaba Khatoon
Editorial Head Glenda Fernandes
Design Head Malavika Talukder

**Language content for Dorling Kindersley by
g-and-w publishing.
Additional translations by
Andiamo! Language Services Ltd.**

This American edition, 2023
First American Edition, 2005
Published in the United States by DK Publishing
1745 Broadway, 20th Floor, New York, NY 10019

A catalog record for this book
is available from the Library of Congress.
ISBN: 978-0-7440-7371-3

DK books are available at special discounts when
purchased in bulk for sales promotions, premiums,
fundraising, or educational use. For details, contact:
DK Publishing Special Markets, 1745 Broadway, 20th
Floor, New York, NY 10019
SpecialSales@dk.com

Printed in China

For the curious

www.dk.com

Contents

How to use this book

Twelve themed chapters are broken down into five daily 15-minute lessons, allowing you to work through four teaching units and one revision unit each week. The lessons cover a range of practical themes, including leisure, business, food and drink, and travel. A reference section at the end contains a menu guide and English-to-French and French-to-English dictionaries.

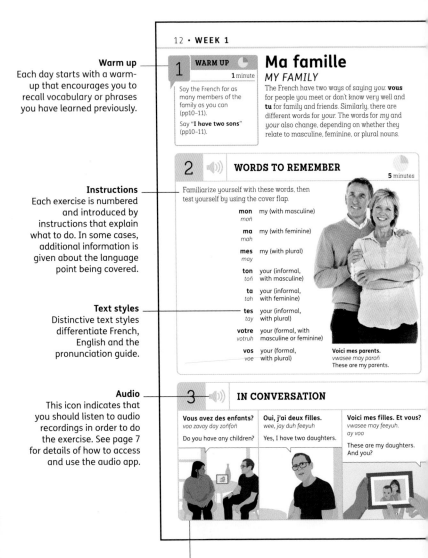

Warm up
Each day starts with a warm-up that encourages you to recall vocabulary or phrases you have learned previously.

12 · WEEK 1

1 WARM UP — 1 minute

Say the French for as many members of the family as you can (pp10–11).

Say "**I have two sons**" (pp10–11).

Ma famille
MY FAMILY

The French have two ways of saying you: **vous** for people you meet or don't know very well and **tu** for family and friends. Similarly, there are different words for your. The words for my and your also change, depending on whether they relate to masculine, feminine, or plural nouns.

2 **WORDS TO REMEMBER** — 5 minutes

Familiarize yourself with these words, then test yourself by using the cover flap.

mon *moñ*	my (with masculine)
ma *mah*	my (with feminine)
mes *may*	my (with plural)
ton *toñ*	your (informal, with masculine)
ta *tah*	your (informal, with feminine)
tes *tay*	your (informal, with plural)
votre *votruh*	your (formal, with masculine or feminine)
vos *voe*	your (formal, with plural)

Voici mes parents.
vwasee may paroñ
These are my parents.

3 **IN CONVERSATION**

Vous avez des enfants?
voo zavay day zoñfoñ

Do you have any children?

Oui, j'ai deux filles.
wee, jay duh feeyuh

Yes, I have two daughters.

Voici mes filles. Et vous?
vwasee may feeyuh. ay voo

These are my daughters. And you?

Instructions
Each exercise is numbered and introduced by instructions that explain what to do. In some cases, additional information is given about the language point being covered.

Text styles
Distinctive text styles differentiate French, English and the pronunciation guide.

Audio
This icon indicates that you should listen to audio recordings in order to do the exercise. See page 7 for details of how to access and use the audio app.

In conversation
Illustrated dialogues reflecting how vocabulary and phrases are used in everyday situations appear throughout the book.

Learn
Keep the flaps open while you learn.

Practice
Use the flaps to cover the answers when you are ready to test yourself.

Conversational tip The French usually ask a question by simply raising the pitch of their voice at the end of a statement—for example, **vous voulez un café?** (*do you want a coffee?*). You could also ask the same question by inverting the verb and subject: **voulez-vous un café?** Or you can use **est-ce que**, a convenient interrogatory phrase that turns a statement into a question, by putting it in front of the sentence like this: **est-ce que vous voulez un café?**

Cultural/Conversational tip
These panels provide additional insights into life in France and language usage.

4 ◄))) USEFUL PHRASES

3 minutes

Learn these phrases, then test yourself by using the cover flap.

	Do you have any brothers? (formal)	**Vous avez des frères?** *voo zavay day frair*
	Do you have any brothers? (informal)	**Tu as des frères?** *tew ah day frair*
	This is my husband.	**Voici mon mari.** *vwasee moñ maree*
	That's my wife.	**C'est ma femme.** *say mah fam*
	Is that your sister? (formal)	**C'est votre sœur?** *say votruh sur*
	Is that your sister? (informal)	**C'est ta sœur?** *say tah sur*

Exercises
Familiarizing you with terms relevant to each topic, these help you build your vocabulary, learn useful phrases, connect words to visuals, and practice what you learn.

4 minutes

J'ai un beau-fils.
jay uñ boe fees

I have a stepson.

5 SAY IT

2 minutes

Do you have any brothers and sisters? (formal)

Do you have any children? (informal)

I have two sisters.

This is my wife.

Time yourself
The icon and text to the right of the heading show you how long you need to spend on each exercise.

Say it
In these exercises, you are asked to apply what you have learned, using different vocabulary.

»

Practice

At the end of every week's lessons, a practice unit lets you test yourself on what you have learned so far. A recap of selected elements from previous lessons helps reinforce your knowledge.

Test yourself
Use the cover flap to conceal the answers while you practice.

Reference

This section appears at the end of the book and brings together all the words and phrases you have learned over the weeks. The menu guide focuses on food and drink, and the dictionary lists French translations of common words and phrases.

Dictionaries
Mini-dictionaries provide ready reference from English to French and French to English for 2,500 words.

Menu guide
Use this guide as a reference for food terminology and popular French dishes.

PRONUNCIATION GUIDE

Many French sounds will already be familiar to you, but a few require special attention. Take note of how these letters are pronounced:

r   a French **r** is pronounced in the back of the throat, producing a sound a little like gargling

j   a French **j** is soft, like the sound in the middle of *pleasure* (as opposed to the hard English *j*, as in *major*)

n   **n** is pronounced nasally when in the combination **on**, **an**, or **in**. Imagine saying *huh* through your nose. The nasal **n** is shown in the pronunciation with this symbol: ñ

ch   **ch** in French is equivalent to *sh* in English, as in *ship*

er/ez   these endings are pronounced *ay*, as in *play*

Pay attention also to these vowel sounds, as they may vary from English:

i   as the English *keep*

au   as the English *over*

eu   as the English *fur*

oi   as the English *wag*

Below each French word or phrase, you will find a pronunciation transcription. Read this, bearing in mind the tips above, and you will achieve a comprehensible result. But remember that the transcription can only ever be an approximation and that there is no real substitute for listening to and mimicking native speakers.

HOW TO USE THE AUDIO APP

The free audio app accompanying this book contains audio recordings for all numbered exercises on the teaching pages, except for the Warm Up and Say It exercises (look out for the audio icon). There is no audio for the revision pages.

To start using the audio with this book, download the **DK 15 Minute Language Course** app on your tablet or smartphone from the App Store or Google Play and select your book from the list of available titles. Please note that this app is not a stand-alone course, but is designed to be used together with the book to familiarize you with the language and provide examples for you to repeat aloud.

There are two ways in which you can use the audio. The first is to read through the 15-minute lessons using just the book, then go back and work with the audio and the book together. Or you can combine the book and the audio from the start, pausing the app to read the instructions on the page.

You are encouraged to listen to the audio and repeat the words and sentences out loud until you are confident you understand and can pronounce what has been said. Remember that repetition is vital for language learning. The more often you listen to a conversation or repeat an oral exercise, the more the new language will sink in.

SUPPORTING AUDIO
This icon indicates that audio recordings are available for you to listen to.

FREE AUDIO APP

1 WARM UP
1 minute

The Warm Up panel appears at the beginning of each topic. Use it to reinforce what you have already learned and to prepare yourself for moving ahead with the new subject.

Bonjour
HELLO

In France, it is part of the culture to greet family and friends with kisses on the cheek. The number of kisses varies from two to four. For example, it is usually three kisses in the south but two in Brittany. In more formal situations, a handshake is part of the normal greeting.

2 WORDS TO REMEMBER
2 minutes

Familiarize yourself with these words by reading them aloud several times, then test yourself by concealing the French on the left with the cover flap.

Bonjour *boñjoor*	Hello
Enchanté (men)/ **Enchantée** (women) *oñshontay*	Pleased to meet you
Bonsoir/Bonne nuit *boñswar/bon nwee*	Good evening/ good night
Au revoir *ovwar*	Goodbye

Salut! *saloo* Hi!

3 IN CONVERSATION: FORMAL
3 minutes

Bonjour. Je m'appelle Céline Legrand.
boñjoor. juh mapell seleen luhgroñ

Hello. My name's Céline Legrand.

Bonjour madame. Monsieur Rossi, enchanté.
boñjoor ma-dam. musyuh rossee, oñshontay

Hello (madam). Mr. Rossi, pleased to meet you.

Enchantée.
oñshontay

Pleased to meet you.

4 PUT INTO PRACTICE

3 minutes

Read the French on the left and follow the instructions to complete this dialogue. Then, test yourself by concealing the French on the right with the cover flap.

	Bonjour monsieur.	**Bonjour madame.**
	boñjoor musyuh	*boñjoor ma-dam*
Hello sir.		
Say: Hello madam.		

	Je m'appelle Isabelle.	**Enchanté.**
	juh mapell eezabel	*oñshontay*
My name is Isabelle.		
Say: Pleased to meet you.		

Cultural tip

The French greet each other with **monsieur** (*sir*) or **madame** (*madam*) much more than English-speakers do. **Mademoiselle** (*miss*) may still be used occasionally in casual speech but the term has been banned from official documents since 2012.

5 USEFUL PHRASES

3 minutes

Learn these phrases by reading them aloud several times, then test yourself by concealing the French on the right with the cover flap.

My name is Jean.	**Je m'appelle Jean.**
	juh mapell joñ
See you soon.	**À bientôt.**
	ah byañtoe
See you tomorrow.	**À demain.**
	ah dumañ
Thank you (very much).	**Merci (beaucoup).**
	mairsee (bohkoo)

6 IN CONVERSATION: INFORMAL

3 minutes

Alors, à demain?	**Oui, au revoir.**	**Au revoir. À bientôt.**
alor, ah dumañ	*wee, ovwar*	*ovwar. ah byañtoe*
So, see you tomorrow?	Yes, goodbye.	Goodbye. See you soon.

Les relations
RELATIVES

Say "**hello**" and "**goodbye**" in French (pp8–9).

Now say "**My name is...**" (pp8–9).

Say "**sir**" and "**madam**" (pp8–9).

In French, the same word is used for two different relationships by marriage: **beau-père** means both father-in-law and stepfather, while **belle-mère** means mother-in-law and stepmother. Similarly, **beau-fils** means son-in-law and stepson, and **belle-fille** is daughter-in-law and stepdaughter.

2 MATCH AND REPEAT

5 minutes

Look at the people in this scene and match their numbers to the vocabulary list on the left. Then, test yourself by concealing the French on the left with the cover flap.

❶ **le père**
luh pair

❷ **la mère**
lah mair

❸ **la sœur**
lah sur

❹ **le frère**
luh frair

❺ **la fille**
lah feeyuh

❻ **le fils**
luh fees

❼ **la grand-mère**
lah groñmair

❽ **le grand-père**
luh groñpair

father ❶　　mother ❷　　sister ❸　　brother ❹

daughter ❺　　son ❻

grandmother ❼　　grandfather ❽

Conversational tip In French, things as well as people are masculine (m) or feminine (f). The French for *the* (singular) is **le** or **la**, and *a/an* is **un** or **une**, depending on whether the word is masculine or feminine. For example, *wine* is masculine (**le vin**), but *car* is feminine (**la voiture**). For plurals, **les** is used for both masculine and feminine. In this book (m) or (f) indicates the gender after a plural.

3 WORDS TO REMEMBER: RELATIVES

4 minutes

la femme
lah fam
wife

le mari
luh maree
husband

Familiarize yourself with these words, then test yourself by using the cover flap.

sister-in-law/stepsister	**la belle-sœur** *lah bell sur*
brother-in-law/ stepbrother	**le beau-frère** *luh boe frair*
half-sister	**la demi-sœur** *lah dumee sur*
half-brother	**le demi-frère** *luh dumee frair*
children	**les enfants** (m) *lay zoñfoñ*
I have four children.	**J'ai quatre enfants.** *jay katruh oñfoñ*
I have two stepdaughters.	**J'ai deux belles-filles.** *jay duh bell feeyuh*

Nous sommes mariés.
noo som mareeay
We are married.

4 WORDS TO REMEMBER: NUMBERS

3 minutes

Familiarize yourself with these words, then test yourself, using the cover flap.

Be careful with the pronunciation of **deux** and **trois**. When you say them before a word that starts with a vowel, you need to say an extra "z" sound—for example, **deux enfants** (*two children*) is pronounced *duh zoñfoñ*, and **trois éclairs** (*three eclairs*), *trwah zayclair*. This is also true of other words.

one	**un/une** *uñ (m)/oon (f)*
two	**deux** *duh*
three	**trois** *trwah*
four	**quatre** *katruh*
five	**cinq** *sank*
six	**six** *sees*
seven	**sept** *set*
eight	**huit** *weet*
nine	**neuf** *nurf*
ten	**dix** *dees*

5 SAY IT

2 minutes

I have five sons.
I have three sisters and a brother.
I have two stepsons.

1 WARM UP

1 minute

Say the French for as many members of the family as you can (pp10–11).

Say "**I have two sons**" (pp10–11).

Ma famille
MY FAMILY

The French have two ways of saying *you*: **vous** for people you meet or don't know very well and **tu** for family and friends. Similarly, there are different words for *your*. The words for *my* and *your* also change, depending on whether they relate to masculine, feminine, or plural nouns.

2 🔊 WORDS TO REMEMBER

5 minutes

Familiarize yourself with these words, then test yourself by using the cover flap.

mon — my (with masculine)
moñ

ma — my (with feminine)
mah

mes — my (with plural)
may

ton — your (informal, with masculine)
toñ

ta — your (informal, with feminine)
tah

tes — your (informal, with plural)
tay

votre — your (formal, with masculine or feminine)
votruh

vos — your (formal, with plural)
voe

Voici mes parents.
vwasee may paroñ
These are my parents.

3 🔊 IN CONVERSATION

Vous avez des enfants?
voo zavay day zoñfoñ

Do you have any children?

Oui, j'ai deux filles.
wee, jay duh feeyuh

Yes, I have two daughters.

Voici mes filles. Et vous?
vwasee may feeyuh.
ay voo

These are my daughters. And you?

Conversational tip The French usually ask a question by simply raising the pitch of their voice at the end of a statement—for example, **vous voulez un café?** (*do you want a coffee?*). You could also ask the same question by inverting the verb and subject: **voulez-vous un café?** Or you can use **est-ce que**, a convenient interrogatory phrase that turns a statement into a question, by putting it in front of the sentence like this: **est-ce que vous voulez un café?**

4 USEFUL PHRASES

3 minutes

Learn these phrases, then test yourself by using the cover flap.

Do you have any brothers? (formal)	**Vous avez des frères?** *voo zavay day frair*
Do you have any brothers? (informal)	**Tu as des frères?** *tew ah day frair*

This is my husband.	**Voici mon mari.** *vwasee moñ maree*
That's my wife.	**C'est ma femme.** *say mah fam*

Is that your sister? (formal)	**C'est votre sœur?** *say votruh sur*
Is that your sister? (informal)	**C'est ta sœur?** *say tah sur*

4 minutes

J'ai un beau-fils.
jay uñ boe fees

I have a stepson.

5 SAY IT

2 minutes

Do you have any brothers and sisters? (formal)

Do you have any children? (informal)

I have two sisters.

This is my wife.

1   WARM UP
1 minute

Say "**See you soon**"
(pp8–9).

Say "**I am married**"
(pp10–11) and "**I have
a daughter**" (pp12–13).

Être et avoir
TO BE AND TO HAVE

There are some essential verbs for you to learn in
this course. You can use them to construct a large
variety of useful phrases. The first two are **être**
(*to be*) and **avoir** (*to have*). Learn them carefully,
as French verbs change more than English ones
according to the pronoun (I, you, etc.) used.

2   ÊTRE: TO BE
5 minutes

Practice **être** (*to be*) and the sample sentences,
then test yourself by using the cover flap.

je suis *juh swee*	I am
tu es *tew ay*	you are (informal singular)
il/elle est *eel/el ay*	he/she is
nous sommes *noo som*	we are
vous êtes *voo zet*	you are (formal singular or plural)
ils/elles sont *eel/el soñ*	they are (m/f)

Je suis anglaise.
juh swee zonglayz
I'm English.

Je suis fatigué. *juh swee fatigay*	I'm tired.
Elle est heureuse? *el ay tururz*	Is she happy?
Nous sommes français. *noo som froñsay*	We're French.

3 AVOIR: TO HAVE

5 minutes

Practice **avoir** (*to have*) and the sample sentences, then test yourself by using the cover flap.

I have	**j'ai** *jay*
you have (informal singular)	**tu as** *tew ah*
he/she has	**il/elle a** *eel/el ah*
we have	**nous avons** *noo zavoñ*
you have (formal singular or plural)	**vous avez** *voo zavay*
they have (m/f)	**ils/elles ont** *eel/el zoñ*

Il a deux baguettes.
eel ah duh baget
He has two baguettes.

He has a meeting.	**Il a un rendez-vous.** *eel ah uñ roñday-voo*
Do you have a cell phone?	**Vous avez un portable?** *voo zavay uñ portabluh*
How many brothers and sisters do you have?	**Vous avez combien de frères et sœurs?** *voo zavay koñbyañ duh frair ay sur*

4 NEGATIVES

4 minutes

To make a sentence negative in French, put **ne** in front of the verb and **pas** just after: **nous ne sommes pas anglais** (*we are not English*). If **ne** is followed by a vowel, it becomes **n'**: **je n'ai pas d'enfants** (*I don't have any children*). But many French people drop the **ne** when they're talking, so you'll just hear **je suis pas** (*I'm not*), **j'ai pas** (*I haven't*), and so on. Read these sentences aloud, then test yourself, using the cover flap.

le vélo
luh vayloe
bicycle

He's not married.	**Il n'est pas marié.** *eel nay pah mariyay*
I am not sure.	**Je ne suis pas sûr(e).** *juh nuh swee pah syur*
We don't have any children.	**Nous n'avons pas d'enfants.** *noo navoñ pah doñfoñ*

Je n'ai pas de voiture.
juh nay pas duh vwatyur
I don't have a car.

Révisez et répétez
REVIEW AND REPEAT

Réponses *Answers*
(Cover with flap)

How many?

❶ **trois**
trwah

❷ **neuf**
nurf

❸ **quatre**
katruh

❹ **deux**
duh

❺ **huit**
weet

❻ **dix**
dees

❼ **cinq**
sank

❽ **sept**
set

❾ **six**
sees

Hello

❶ **Bonjour. Je m'appelle... [your name].**
boñjoor. juh mapell...

❷ **Enchanté(e).**
oñshontay

❸ **Oui, et j'ai deux fils. Et vous?**
wee, ay jay duh fees. ay voo

❹ **Au revoir. À demain.**
ovwar. ah dumañ

---

1   HOW MANY?
2 minutes

Say these numbers in French, then test yourself by using the cover flap.

---

2   HELLO
4 minutes

You meet someone in a formal situation. Join in the conversation, replying in French following the numbered English prompts.

Bonjour. Je m'appelle Nicole.
❶ Hello. My name is... [your name].

Voici mon mari, Henri.
❷ Pleased to meet you.

Vous êtes marié(e)?
❸ Yes, and I have two sons. And you?

Nous avons trois filles.
❹ Goodbye. See you tomorrow.

Réponses *Answers*
(Cover with flap)

3 BE OR HAVE
5 minutes

Fill in the blanks with the correct form of **avoir** (*to have*) or **être** (*to be*).

❶ Je _____ anglaise.

❷ Nous _____ quatre enfants.

❸ Elle _____ une belle-fille.

❹ Nous _____ français.

❺ Vous _____ rendez-vous?

❻ Il n' _____ pas fatigué.

❼ Je n' _____ pas de portable.

❽ Nous _____ mariés.

Be or have
❶ **suis**
swee

❷ **avons**
avoñ

❸ **a**
ah

❹ **sommes**
som

❺ **avez**
avay

❻ **est**
ay

❼ **ai**
ay

❽ **sommes**
som

4 RELATIVES
4 minutes

Name these family members in French.

grandmother ❶   grandfather ❷
❸ father   ❹ mother
sister ❺   brother ❻
daughter ❼   ❽ son

Relatives
❶ **la grand-mère**
lah groñmair

❷ **le grand-père**
luh groñpair

❸ **le père**
luh pair

❹ **la mère**
lah mair

❺ **la sœur**
lah sur

❻ **le frère**
luh frair

❼ **la fille**
lah feeyuh

❽ **le fils**
luh fees

1 WARM UP

1 minute

Count to ten (pp10–11).

Remind yourself how to say "**hello**" and "**goodbye**" (pp8–9).

Ask "**Do you have a baguette?**" (pp14–15).

Au café
IN THE CAFÉ

In a French **café**, you can get coffee and croissants in the morning. Most cafés now also serve food, although it tends to be small plates or snacks rather than full meals. You can either sit at the counter or have table service. It is usual to tip the server, but a good rounding up will be enough.

2 ◀)) WORDS TO REMEMBER

Familiarize yourself with these words, then test yourself by using the cover flap.

le café crème
luh kafay krem
coffee with milk

le grand café
luh groñ kafay
large black coffee

le thé
luh tay
black tea

le thé au lait
luh tay oh lay
tea with milk

le café
luh cafeh
small black coffee

la confiture
lah coñfeetyur
jam

le sucre
luh sookruh
sugar

3 ◀)) IN CONVERSATION

Bonjour. Je voudrais un café crème, s'il vous plaît.
bonjoor. juh voodray uñ kafay krem, seel voo play

Hello. I would like coffee with milk, please.

C'est tout, madame?
say too ma-dam

Is that all, madam?

Vous avez des croissants?
voo zavay day krossoñ

Do you have any croissants?

Cultural tip A standard coffee is small and black. You'll need to ask if you want it any other way. If you like milk in your tea, you'll need to specify cold milk (**lait froid**); otherwise, you are likely to get a jug of hot milk.

5 minutes

le pain
luh pañ
bread

Learn these phrases, then test yourself by using the cover flap.

Je voudrais un grand café, s'il vous plaît.
juh voodray uñ groñ kafay, seel voo play

I'd like a large black coffee, please.

C'est tout?
say too

Is that all?

Je vais prendre un croissant.
juh vay proñdruh uñ krossoñ

I'll have a croissant.

C'est combien?
say koñbyañ

How much is that?

4 minutes

Oui, bien sûr.
wee, byañ syur

Yes, certainly.

Alors deux croissants. C'est combien?
alor duh krossoñ. say koñbyañ

Two croissants then. How much is that?

Huit euros, s'il vous plaît.
weet uroh, seel voo play

Eight euros, please.

WARM UP

1 minute

Say "**I'd like**" (pp18–19).

Say "**I don't have a brother**" (pp14–15).

Ask "**Do you have any croissants?**" (pp18–19).

Au restaurant
IN THE RESTAURANT

There are a variety of eating places in France. A **café** will serve drinks and small plates (pp18–19). A **brasserie** is a traditional restaurant: the service is fast, and there's usually no need to book. In a more formal gastronomic **restaurant**, it's necessary to make a reservation and to dress nicely.

  MATCH AND REPEAT

5 minutes

Match the numbered items to the list, then test yourself, using the cover flap.

❶ **la soucoupe**
lah sookoop

❷ **la tasse**
lah tass

❸ **le verre**
luh vair

❹ **la fourchette**
lah forshet

❺ **le couteau**
luh kootoe

❻ **la cuillère**
lah kweeyair

❼ **l'assiette** (f)
lasyet

❽ **la serviette**
lah sairvyet

cup ❷ glass ❸ saucer ❶ ❹ fork ❻ spoon knife ❺ plate ❼ napkin ❽

  IN CONVERSATION

Bonjour. Je voudrais une table pour quatre.
boñjoor. juh voodray oon tabluh poor katruh

Hello. I would like a table for four.

Vous avez une réservation?
voo zavay oon raysairvasyoñ

Do you have a reservation?

Oui, au nom de Smith.
wee, oh noñ duh Smith

Yes, in the name of Smith.

4 WORDS TO REMEMBER

3 minutes

Familiarize yourself with these words, then test yourself, using the cover flap.

menu	**la carte** *lah kart*
wine list	**la carte des vins** *lah kart day vañ*
starters	**les entrées** (f) *lay zontray*
main courses	**les plats** (m) *lay plah*
desserts	**les desserts** (m) *lay dessair*
breakfast	**le petit-déjeuner** *luh puhtee dayjunay*
lunch	**le déjeuner** *luh dayjunay*
dinner	**le dîner** *luh deenay*

Je déjeune avec ma famille.
juh dayjuñ avek mah fameeyuh
I'm having lunch with my family.

5 USEFUL PHRASES

2 minutes

Learn these phrases, then test yourself, using the cover flap.

What do you have for dessert?	**Qu'est ce que vous avez comme dessert?** *keskuh voo zavay kom dessair*
The bill, please.	**L'addition, s'il vous plaît.** *ladeesyoñ, seel voo play*

4 minutes

D'accord. Quelle table préférez-vous? *dakor. kel tabluh prayfayray voo*	**Près de la fenêtre, s'il vous plaît.** *pray duh lah fenetruh, seel voo play*	**Mais bien sûr. Suivez-moi.** *may byañ syur. sweevay mwah*
Fine. Which table would you like?	Near the window, please.	But of course. Follow me.

Les plats
DISHES

<table>
<tr><td>

1

WARM UP

1 minute

Say "**I'm tired**" and "**I'm not sure**" (pp14–15).

Ask "**Do you have a fork?**" (pp20–21).

Say "**I'd like a white coffee**" (pp18–19).

</td></tr>
</table>

France is famous for its cuisine and the quality of its restaurants. It also offers a wide variety of regional dishes. Plenty of garlic and butter are a feature of many typical dishes. Although French cuisine is traditionally meat-based, many restaurants now offer a vegetarian menu.

---

2 **MATCH AND REPEAT**

4 minutes

Match the numbered items to the list, then test yourself, using the cover flap.

❶ **les légumes** (m)
lay laygoom

❷ **le fruit**
luh froo-wee

❸ **le fromage**
luh fromarj

❹ **les noix** (f)
lay nwah

❺ **la soupe**
lah soop

❻ **la volaille**
lah vol-eye

❼ **les pâtes** (f)
lay pat

❽ **le poisson**
luh pwassoñ

❾ **les fruits de mer** (m)
lay froo-wee duh mair

❿ **la viande**
lah vee-ond

❶ vegetables   fruit ❷

❸ cheese

nuts ❹   soup ❺

❻ poultry

pasta ❼

fish ❽   ❾ seafood   meat ❿

Cultural tip You will usually have the choice of eating a set **menu** or ordering **à la carte**. With a set menu, you usually have to choose between an appetizer and a dessert. Bread for the table comes as standard.

3 WORDS TO REMEMBER: COOKING METHODS

3 minutes

Familiarize yourself with these words, then test yourself, using the cover flap.

fried	**frit(e)**
	free(t)
grilled	**grillé(e)**
	greeyay
roasted	**rôti(e)**
	rotee
boiled	**bouilli(e)**
	booyee
steamed	**à la vapeur**
	ah lah vapur
rare	**saignant(e)**
	say-nyoñ(t)

Je voudrais mon steak bien cuit.
juh voodray moñ stayk byañ kwee
I'd like my steak well done.

4 WORDS TO REMEMBER: DRINKS

3 minutes

Familiarize yourself with these words, then test yourself, using the cover flap.

water	**l'eau** (f)
	loe
still water	**l'eau plate** (f)
	loe plat
wine	**le vin**
	luh vañ
beer	**la bière**
	lah biyair
fruit juice	**le jus de fruits**
	luh joo duh froo-wee

l'eau gazeuse
loe gazuz
fizzy water

5 USEFUL PHRASES

2 minutes

Learn these phrases, then test yourself, using the cover flap.

I'm a vegetarian.	**Je suis végétarien(ne).**
	juh swee vejitah-ryañ(en)
I'm allergic to nuts.	**Je suis allergique aux noix.**
	juh swee zalurzheek oh nwah
What are "escargots"?	**Qu'est que c'est les "escargots"?**
	keskuh say lay zeskargoh

6 SAY IT

2 minutes

What is "cassoulet"?

I'm allergic to seafood.

I'd like a beer.

1 WARM UP
1 minute

What are "**breakfast**," "**lunch**," and "**dinner**" in French? (pp20–21).

Say "**I**," "**you**" (informal), "**he**," "**she**," "**we**," "**you**" (plural/formal), "**they**" (masculine), "**they**" (feminine) (pp14–15).

Vouloir
TO WANT

In this section, you will learn the present tense of a verb that is essential to everyday conversation—**vouloir** (*to want*)—as well as a useful polite form, **je voudrais** (*I would like*). Remember to use this form when requesting something, because **je veux** (*I want*) may sound too strong.

2 **VOULOIR**: TO WANT
6 minutes

Practice **vouloir** (*to want*) and the sample sentences, then test yourself by using the cover flap.

je veux *juh vuh*	I want
tu veux *tew vuh*	you want (informal singular)
il/elle veut *eel/el vuh*	he/she wants
nous voulons *noo vooloñ*	we want
vous voulez *voo voolay*	you want (formal singular or plural)
ils/elles veulent *eel/el verl*	they want (m/f)

Tu veux du vin? *tew vuh dew vañ*	Do you want some wine?
Elle veut une nouvelle voiture. *el vuh oon noovel vwatyur*	She wants a new car.
Nous voulons aller en vacances. *noo vooloñ zallay oñ vakons*	We want to go on vacation.

Je veux des bonbons.
juh vuh day boñ-boñ
I want some candy.

Conversational tip To say *some*, **de** (*of*) combines with **le**, **la**, or **les** to produce **du** for the masculine, **de la** for the feminine, or **des** for the plural, as in **du café**, **de la confiture**, and **des citrons** (*lemons*). If the sentence is negative, use only **de**, as in **il n'y a pas de café**. In the same way, **à** (*to*) combines with **le**, **la**, or **les** to produce **au** for the masculine, **à la** for the feminine, and **aux** for the plural.

3 POLITE REQUESTS

4 minutes

There is a form of **je veux** (*I want*) used for polite requests: **je voudrais** (*I would like*). Practice the sample sentences, then test yourself by using the cover flap.

I'd like a beer, please.

Je voudrais une bière, s'il vous plaît.
juh voodray oon biyair, seel voo play

I'd like a table for tonight.

Je voudrais une table pour ce soir.
juh voodray oon tabluh poor suh swar

I'd like the menu.

Je voudrais la carte.
juh voodray lah kart

4 PUT INTO PRACTICE

4 minutes

Complete this dialogue, then test yourself, using the cover flap.

Bonsoir, madame. Vous avez une réservation?
boñswar, ma-dam. Voo zavay oon raysairvasyoñ

Good evening, madam. Do you have a reservation?

Say: No, but I would like a table for three, please.

Non, mais je voudrais une table pour trois, s'il vous plaît.
noñ, may juh voodray oon tabluh poor trwah, seel voo play

Quelle table préférez-vous?
kel tabluh prayfayray voo

Which table would you like?

Say: Near the window, please.

Près de la fenêtre, s'il vous plaît.
pray duh lah fenetruh, seel voo play

Révisez et répétez
REVIEW AND REPEAT

Réponses *Answers*
(Cover with flap)

At the table

❶ les noix
lay nwah

❷ le sucre
luh sookruh

❸ les fruits de mer
lay froo-wee duh mair

❹ la viande
lah vee-ond

❺ le verre
luh vair

---

1 AT THE TABLE

Name these items in French.

 ❶ nuts

 sugar ❷

❸ seafood

meat ❹

glass ❺

This is my…

❶ C'est mon mari.
say moñ maree

❷ Voici ma fille.
vwasee mah feeyuh

❸ Mes enfants sont fatigués.
may zoñfoñ soñ fatigay

❹ Ma table est en terrasse.
mah tabluh ay toñ terass

---

2 THIS IS MY…

4 minutes

Say these sentences in French.
Use **mon**, **ma**, or **mes**.

❶ This is my husband.
❷ Here is my daughter.
❸ My children are tired.
❹ My table is on the terrace.

I'd like…

❶ Je voudrais un café.
juh voodray uñ kafay

❷ Je voudrais de la confiture.
juh voodray duh lah coñfeetyur

❸ Je voudrais du pain.
juh voodray doo pañ

❹ Je voudrais un café crème.
juh voodray uñ kafay krem

---

3 I'D LIKE…

3 minutes

Say that you'd like these items in French.

black coffee ❶   jam ❷   bread ❸   coffee with milk ❹

⑥ pasta

⑦ cheese

knife ⑧

⑨ napkin

⑩ beer

4 minutes

At the table

⑥ **les pâtes**
lay pat

⑦ **le fromage**
luh fromarj

⑧ **le couteau**
luh kootoe

⑨ **la serviette**
lah sairvyet

⑩ **la bière**
lah biyair

4 RESTAURANT

4 minutes

You arrive at a restaurant. Join in the conversation, replying in French following the numbered English prompts.

Bonjour madame, monsieur.
❶ Hello. I would like a table for six.

Vous avez une réservation?
❷ Yes, in the name of Beauvoir.

Suivez-moi, s'il vous plaît.
❸ I'd like the menu, please.

Et vous voulez la carte des vins?
❹ No. Fizzy water, please.

Voilà.
❺ I don't have a glass.

Restaurant

❶ **Bonjour. Je voudrais une table pour six.**
boñjoor. juh voodray oon tabluh por sees

❷ **Oui, au nom de Beauvoir.**
wee, oh noñ duh boe-vwa

❸ **Je voudrais la carte, s'il vous plaît.**
juh voodray lah kart, seel voo play

❹ **Non. De l'eau gazeuse, s'il vous plaît.**
noñ. duh loe gazuz, seel voo play

❺ **Je n'ai pas de verre.**
juh nay pah duh vair

Les jours et les mois
DAYS AND MONTHS

In French, the days of the week (**les jours de la semaine**) and months of the year (**les mois de l'année**) do not have capital letters. The months have similar names to the English. You use **en** with months—**en avril** (*in April*)—but not with days.

---

2 **WORDS TO REMEMBER:** DAYS

5 minutes

Familiarize yourself with these words, then test yourself, using the cover flap.

lundi *luñdee*	Monday
mardi *mardee*	Tuesday
mercredi *mairkrudee*	Wednesday
jeudi *jurdee*	Thursday
vendredi *voñdrudee*	Friday
samedi *samdee*	Saturday
dimanche *deemonsh*	Sunday
aujourd'hui *oh-joordwee*	today
demain *dumañ*	tomorrow
hier *eeyair*	yesterday

Demain, c'est lundi.
dumañ, say luñdee
Tomorrow is Monday.

---

3 **USEFUL PHRASES**: DAYS

2 minutes

Learn these phrases, then test yourself by using the cover flap.

La réunion n'est pas mardi.
lah rayoonyoñ nay pah mardee
The meeting isn't on Tuesday.

Je travaille le dimanche.
juh trav-eye luh deemonsh
I work on Sundays.

4 WORDS TO REMEMBER: MONTHS

5 minutes

Familiarize yourself with these words, then test yourself, using the cover flap.

Notre anniversaire de mariage est en juillet.
notruh aneevairsair duh mareeaj ay toñ jweeyay
Our wedding anniversary is in July.

Noël est en décembre.
nowel ay toñ daysombruh
Christmas is in December.

January	**janvier**	*joñvyay*
February	**février**	*fevreeyay*
March	**mars**	*mars*
April	**avril**	*avreel*
May	**mai**	*may*
June	**juin**	*jwañ*
July	**juillet**	*jweeyay*
August	**août**	*oot*
September	**septembre**	*septombruh*
October	**octobre**	*oktobruh*
November	**novembre**	*novombruh*
December	**décembre**	*daysombruh*
month	**le mois**	*luh mwah*
year	**l'an/l'année** (m/f)	*loñ/lannay*

5 USEFUL PHRASES: MONTHS

2 minutes

Learn these phrases, then test yourself, using the cover flap.

My children are on vacation in August.

Mes enfants sont en vacances en août.
may zoñfoñ soñ toñ vakons oñ oot

My birthday is in June.

Mon anniversaire est en juin.
moñ naneevairsair ay toñ jwañ

L'heure et les nombres
TIME AND NUMBERS

<table>
<tr><td>

1 **WARM UP**

1 minute

Count in French from 1 to 10 (pp10–11).

Say "**I have a reservation**" (pp20–21).

Say "**The meeting is on Wednesday**" (pp28–29).

</td><td>

The 12-hour clock is used in everyday speech, while the 24-hour clock is employed at stations, airports, and so forth. In English the minutes come first (ten to five); in French the hour comes first: **cinq heures moins dix** (*five minus ten*).

</td></tr>
</table>

---

2 **WORDS TO REMEMBER**: TIME

4 minutes

Familiarize yourself with these words, then test yourself by using the cover flap.

une heure *oon ur*	one o'clock
une heure cinq *oon ur sank*	five past one
une heure et quart *oon ur ay kar*	quarter past one
une heure vingt *oon ur vañ*	twenty past one
une heure et demie *oon ur ay dumee*	half past one
deux heures moins le quart *duh zur mwañ luh kar*	quarter to two
deux heures moins dix *duh zur mwañ dees*	ten to two

---

3 **USEFUL PHRASES**

2 minutes

Learn these phrases, then test yourself by using the cover flap.

Quelle heure est-il? *kel ur ay teel*	What time is it?
À quelle heure voulez-vous le petit déjeuner? *ah kel ur voolay voo luh puhtee dayjunay*	What time do you want breakfast?
J'ai une réservation pour douze heures. *jay oon raysairvasyoñ poor dooz ur*	I have a reservation for twelve o'clock.

4 WORDS TO REMEMBER:
HIGHER NUMBERS

6 minutes

In French, when you say 21, 31, etc., you say **vingt-et-un**, **trente-et-un**, and so on. After that, just put the numbers together without **et**: **vingt-deux** (22), **quarante-cinq** (45).

70 is **soixante-dix** (*sixty-ten*), 75 is **soixante-quinze** (*sixty-fifteen*), and so on. **Quatre-vingt** (80) means *four-twenties*, and 90 is **quatre-vingt-dix** (*four-twenties-ten*). So 82 is **quatre-vingt-deux**, and 97 is **quatre-vingt-dix-sept**.

Familiarize yourself with these words, then test yourself, using the cover flap.

J'ai payé quatre-vingt-cinq euros par paiement sans contact.
jay payay katruh-vañ-sank uroh par paymoñ soñ kontakt
I've paid eighty-five euros by contactless payment.

eleven	**onze**	*onz*
twelve	**douze**	*dooz*
thirteen	**treize**	*trez*
fourteen	**quatorze**	*katorz*
fifteen	**quinze**	*kanz*
sixteen	**seize**	*sez*
seventeen	**dix-sept**	*deeset*
eighteen	**dix-huit**	*deezweet*
nineteen	**dix-neuf**	*deeznurf*
twenty	**vingt**	*vañ*
thirty	**trente**	*tront*
forty	**quarante**	*karont*
fifty	**cinquante**	*sankont*
sixty	**soixante**	*swasont*
seventy	**soixante-dix**	*swasont-dees*
eighty	**quatre-vingts**	*katruh-vañ*
ninety	**quatre-vingt-dix**	*katruh-vañ-dees*
hundred	**cent**	*soñ*
three hundred	**trois-cents**	*trwah soñ*
thousand	**mille**	*meel*
ten thousand	**dix mille**	*dee meel*
two hundred thousand	**deux-cent mille**	*duh soñ meel*
one million	**un million**	*oon meel-yoñ*

5 SAY IT

2 minutes

twenty-five

sixty-eight

eighty-four

ninety-one

five to ten

half past eleven

What time is lunch?

1 WARM UP

1 minute

Say the days of the week in French (pp28–29).

Say "**It's three o'clock**" (pp30–31).

What's the French for "**today**," "**tomorrow**," and "**yesterday**"? (pp28–29).

Les rendez-vous
APPOINTMENTS

Business in France is generally conducted more formally than in Britain or the United States; always address business contacts as **vous** (formal *you*). The French tend to leave the office for the lunch hour, often having a sit-down meal in a restaurant or, less commonly, at home.

2 USEFUL PHRASES

5 minutes

Learn these phrases, then test yourself, using the cover flap.

Prenons rendez-vous pour demain.
prunoñ ronday-voo poor dumañ
Let's meet tomorrow.

Avec qui?
avek kee
With whom?

Quand êtes-vous libre?
koñ et-voo leebruh
When are you free?

Je suis désolé(e), je suis occupé(e).
juh swee dayzolay, juh swee zokupay
I'm sorry, I'm busy.

Pourquoi pas jeudi?
poorkwah pah jurdee
How about Thursday?

C'est bon pour moi.
say boh poor mwah
That's good for me.

Bienvenue.
byañvenoo
Welcome.

la poignée de main
lah pwanyay duh mañ
handshake

3 IN CONVERSATION

Bonjour. J'ai rendez-vous.
boñjoor. jay ronday-voo

Hello. I have an appointment.

Avec qui?
avek kee

With whom?

Avec Monsieur Leblanc.
avek musyuh luh bloñ

With Mr. Leblanc.

MAKING ARRANGEMENTS · 33

4 PUT INTO PRACTICE

5 minutes

Complete this dialogue, then test yourself, using the cover flap.

Prenons rendez-vous pour jeudi.
prunoñ ronday-voo poor jurdee

Let's meet on Thursday.

Say: Sorry, I'm busy.

Je suis désolé, je suis occupé.
juh swee dayzolay, juh swee zokupay

Quand êtes-vous libre?
koñ et-voo leebruh

When are you free?

Say: Tuesday afternoon.

Mardi après-midi.
mardee apray meedee

C'est bon pour moi.
say boñ poor mwa

That's good for me.

Ask: What time?

À quelle heure?
ah kel ur

À quatre heures, si c'est bon pour vous.
ah katruh ur see say boñ poor voo

At four o'clock, if that's good for you.

Say: It's good for me.

C'est bon pour moi.
say boñ poor mwah

---

4 minutes

Très bien. À quelle heure?
tray byañ. ah kel ur

Very good. What time?

À trois heures, mais je suis un peu en retard.
ah trwah zur, may juh swee uñ puh oñ retar

At three o'clock, but I'm a little late.

Ne vous inquiétez pas. Asseyez-vous, je vous en prie.
nuh voo zañkyetay pah. assayay voo, juh voo zoñ pree

Don't worry. Sit down, please.

1 WARM UP
1 minute

Say "**I'm sorry**" (pp32–33).

What is the French for "**I'd like an appointment**"? (pp32–33).

How do you say "**With whom?**" in French? (pp32–33).

Au téléphone
ON THE TELEPHONE

The emergency number for police, ambulance, or fire services across the European Union is 112. You can dial it free of charge from cell phones or landlines anywhere in the EU. To make direct international calls from France, dial the access code 00 followed by the country code, area code (omit the initial 0), and then the phone number. The country code for France is 33.

2 MATCH AND REPEAT

Match the numbered items to the list, then test yourself, using the cover flap.

❶ earphones ❷ headphones

❶ **les écouteurs** (m)
lay zaykootur

❷ **le casque**
luh kask

❹ cell phone

❸ **le téléphone**
luh telayfon

❹ **le portable**
luh portabluh

❻ SIM card

❺ charger

❺ **le chargeur**
luh sharjur

❻ **la carte SIM**
lah kart seem

112

❼ **le répondeur**
luh raypoñdur

Je voudrais acheter une carte SIM.
juh voodray ashuhtay oon kart seem
I'd like to buy a SIM card.

3 IN CONVERSATION

Allô. Pauline Dubois à l'appareil.
aloh. pawleen doo bwah ah lap-paray

Hello. Pauline Dubois speaking.

Bonjour. Je voudrais parler à Rachid Djamal.
boñjoor. juh voodray parlay ah rasheed jahmal

Hello. I'd like to speak to Rachid Djamal.

C'est de la part de qui?
say duh lah par duh kee

May I know who's calling?

5 SAY IT
2 minutes

I'd like to speak to
Mr. Hachart.

Can I leave a message
for Emma?

Can she call me back on
Wednesday, please?

4 USEFUL PHRASES
4 minutes

Learn these phrases, then test yourself,
using the cover flap.

I'd like the number
for Michel.

**Je voudrais le numéro
de Michel.**
*juh voodray luh noomairoe
duh meeshell*

I'd like to speak to
Françoise Martin.

**Je voudrais parler à
Françoise Martin.**
*juh voodray parlay ah
franswahz martañ*

Can I leave a
message?

**Je peux laisser
un message?**
*juh puh laysay
uñ mesarj*

Sorry, I have the
wrong number.

**Désolé, je me suis
trompé de numéro.**
*dayzolay, juh muh swee
trompay duh noomairoe*

4 minutes

❸ telephone

answering machine ❼

4 minutes

Jean Leblanc de l'imprimerie Laporte. *joñ luhbloñ duh lahpreemuree laport*	**Désolée. La ligne est occupée.** *dayzolay. lah leenyuh et okupay*	**Il peut me rappeler, s'il vous plaît?** *eel puh muh raplay, seel voo play*
Jean Leblanc of Laporte Printers.	I'm sorry. The line is busy.	Can he call me back, please?

Révisez et répétez
REVIEW AND REPEAT

Telephones

❶ **le portable**
luh portabluh

❷ **le téléphone**
luh telayfon

❸ **le répondeur**
luh raypoñdur

❹ **le casque**
luh kask

❺ **la carte SIM**
lah kart seem

When?

❶ **I have a meeting on Monday, May 20.**

❷ **My birthday is in September.**

❸ **I come back on Sunday.**

❹ **They don't work in August.**

Time

❶ **une heure**
oon ur

❷ **une heure cinq**
oon ur sank

❸ **une heure et quart**
oon ur ay kar

❹ **une heure vingt**
oon ur vañ

❺ **une heure et demie**
oon ur ay dumee

❻ **deux heures moins dix**
duh zur mwañ dees

---

1 · TELEPHONES

Name these items in French.

❶ cell phone
❷ telephone
❸ answering machine
headphones ❹

---

2 · WHEN?

2 minutes

What do these sentences mean?

❶ J'ai rendez-vous lundi vingt mai.
❷ Mon anniversaire est en septembre.
❸ Je reviens dimanche.
❹ Ils ne travaillent pas en août.

---

3 · TIME

3 minutes

Say these times in French.

❶ ❷ ❸
❹ ❺ ❻

Réponses *Answers*
(Cover with flap)

3 minutes

5 SIM card

4 SUMS

4 minutes

Say the answers to these sums in French.

❶ 10 + 6 = ?
❷ 14 + 25 = ?
❸ 66 − 13 = ?
❹ 40 + 34 = ?
❺ 90 + 9 = ?
❻ 46 − 5 = ?

Réponses *Answers*
(Cover with flap)

Sums

❶ seize
sez

❷ trente-neuf
tront-nurf

❸ cinquante-trois
sankont-trwah

❹ soixante-quatorze
swasont-katorz

**❺ quatre-vingt
dix-neuf**
katruh-vañ deeznuf

❻ quarante-et-un
karont-ay-uñ

5 I WANT...

3 minutes

Fill in the blanks with the correct form of **vouloir** (*to want*).

❶ Vous ____ un café?
❷ Elle ____ aller en vacances.
❸ Nous ____ une table pour trois.
❹ Tu ____ une bière?
❺ Je ____ une nouvelle voiture.
❻ Il ____ des bonbons.

I want...

❶ voulez
voolay

❷ veut
vuh

❸ voulons
vooloñ

❹ veux
vuh

❺ veux
vuh

❻ veut
vuh

1 **WARM UP**

1 minute

Count to 100 in tens
(pp10–11, pp30–31).

Ask "**At what time?**"
(pp30–31).

Say "**It's half-past one**"
(pp30–31).

Au guichet
AT THE TICKET OFFICE

In France, before getting on the train, you must
validate (**composter**) your ticket by stamping it.
Special yellow machines are installed in every
railway station for this purpose. Fines are handed
out to those who forget to validate their tickets.
Most trains have both first- and second-class seats.

---

2 **WORDS TO REMEMBER**

3 minutes

Familiarize yourself with these words, then
test yourself, using the cover flap.

la gare *lah gar*	station
le train *luh trañ*	train
la voiture *lah vwatyur*	carriage
le billet *luh beeyay*	ticket
aller-simple *allay-sañpluh*	single
aller-retour *allay-rutoor*	return
première classe *prumyair klas*	first class
seconde classe *sugond klas*	second class

le passager
luh pasahjay
passenger

le quai
luh kay
platform

La gare est pleine de monde.
lah gar ay plen duh moñd
The station is crowded.

---

3 **IN CONVERSATION**

**Deux billets pour
Bordeaux s'il vous plaît.**
*duh beeyay poor bordoe
seel voo play*

Two tickets for
Bordeaux, please.

Aller-retour?
allay rutoor

Return?

**Oui. Je dois réserver
des places?**
*wee. juh dwah rayzurvay
day plas*

Yes. Do I need to
reserve seats?

4 USEFUL PHRASES

5 minutes

Learn these phrases, then test yourself, using the cover flap.

Le train pour Poitiers est annulé.
luh trañ poor pwatyer et anulay
The train for Poitiers is canceled.

How much is a ticket to Lille?	**C'est combien un billet pour Lille?** *say koñbyañ uñ beeyay poor leel*
Do you accept credit cards?	**Vous acceptez la carte?** *voo zakseptay lah kart*
Do I have to change trains?	**Je dois changer de train?** *juh dwah shonjay duh trañ*
Which platform does the train leave from?	**Le train part de quel quai?** *luh trañ par duh kel kay*
Are there discounts?	**Vous faites des réductions?** *voo fet day raydooksyoñ*
What time does the train for Paris leave?	**À quelle heure part le train pour Paris?** *ah kel ur par luh trañ poor paree*

Cultural tip Most large railway stations have ticket offices and automatic ticket machines that accept credit and debit cards, cash, and payments via mobile and digital wallets.

5 SAY IT

2 minutes

Which platform does the train for Paris leave from?

Three tickets to Lyon, please.

---

4 minutes

Ce n'est pas nécessaire. Trois-cents euros s'il vous plaît.
suh nay pah nesaysair. trwah soñ uroh seel voo play

That's not necessary. Three hundred euros, please.

Vous acceptez la carte?
voo zakseptay lah kart

Do you accept credit cards?

Bien sûr. Le train part du quai numéro cinq.
byañ syur. luh trañ par doo kay noomairoe sank

Certainly. The train leaves from platform five.

<table>
<tr><td>

1

</td><td>

WARM UP

1 minute

How do you say "**train**" in French? (pp38–39).

What does "**Le train part de quel quai?**" mean? (pp38–39).

Ask "**When are you free?**" (pp32–33).

</td></tr>
</table>

Aller et prendre
TO GO AND TO TAKE

Aller (*to go*) and **prendre** (*to take*) are essential verbs in French. You can also use **prendre** to say *I'll have* (**je prends**) when you talk about food and drink. Note that the present tense in French includes the sense of a continuous action—for example, **je vais** means both *I go* and *I am going*.

---

2 🔊 **ALLER:** TO GO

 6 minutes

Practise **aller** (*to go*) and the sample sentences, then test yourself, using the cover flap.

je vais *juh vay*	I go
tu vas *tew vah*	you go (informal singular)
il/elle va *eel/el vah*	he/she goes
nous allons *noo zalloñ*	we go
vous allez *voo zallay*	you go (formal singular or plural)
ils/elles vont *eel/el voñ*	they go (m/f)

Où allez-vous? *oo allay voo*	Where are you going?
Je vais à Paris. *juh vay zah paree*	I'm going to Paris.
Nous allons à l'école en train. *noo zalloñ ah laykoloñ trañ*	We go to school by train.

Je vais à la Tour Eiffel.
juh vay zah lah toor eefel
I'm going to the Eiffel Tower.

Cultural tip The **TGV (train à grande vitesse)** is a fast train that can get you from Paris to the south of France in under three hours. Generally, you will need to reserve a seat. **TER (trains express régionaux)** is another type of fast train. These trains are cheaper—and generally slower—than the **TGV**. You can buy a ticket on the day of travel and get on without a reservation.

3 PRENDRE: TO TAKE

6 minutes

Practice **prendre** (*to take*) and the sample sentences, then test yourself, using the cover flap.

je prends *juh proñ*	I take
tu prends *tew proñ*	you take (informal singular)
il/elle prend *eel/el proñ*	he/she takes
nous prenons *noo prunoñ*	we take
vous prenez *voo prunay*	you take (formal singular or plural)
ils/elles prennent *eel/el pren*	they take (m/f)

Je prends le métro tous les jours.
juh proñ luh metroe too lay joor
I take the metro every day.

Je ne veux pas prendre un taxi.
juh nuh vuh pah proñdruh uñ taksee

I don't want to take a taxi.

Prenez la première à gauche.
prunay lah prumyair ah gaush

Take the first on the left.

Il va prendre le bœuf bourguignon.
eel vah proñdruh luh buf boorgheenyoñ

He'll have the beef bourguignon.

4 PUT INTO PRACTICE

2 minutes

Complete this dialogue, then test yourself, using the cover flap.

Où allez-vous?
oo allay voo

Where are you going?

Say: I'm going to the Louvre.

Je vais au Louvre.
juh vay zoh loovruh

Vous voulez prendre le métro?
voo voolay proñdruh luh metroe

Do you want to take the metro?

Say: No, I want to go by bus.

Non, je veux y aller en bus.
noñ. juh vuh ee allay oñ boos

Taxi, bus et métro
TAXI, BUS, AND METRO

1 WARM UP

1 minute

Say "**I'd like to go to the station**" (pp40–41).

Ask "**Where are you going?**" (pp40–41).

Say "**fruit**" and "**cheese**" (pp22–23).

It's unusual to flag down a taxi in the street – you need to find one of the many taxi areas and wait there. With buses, as with trains, you need to validate your ticket in a machine at the time of travel. For the metro, you can buy a single fare, or you can get a Navigo pass at almost any metro, RER, or Transilien ticket window.

2 **WORDS TO REMEMBER**

4 minutes

Familiarize yourself with these words, then test yourself, using the cover flap.

le bus *luh boos*	bus
le car *luh kar*	coach
la gare routière *lah gar rootyair*	bus station
l'arrêt de bus (m) *laray duh boos*	bus stop
le tarif *luh tareef*	fare
le taxi *luh taksee*	taxi
la rangée de taxis *lah roñjay duh taksee*	taxi rank
la station de métro *lah stasyoñ duh metroe*	metro station

Le bus numéro 4 s'arrête ici?
luh boos noomairoe katruh saret eesee
Does the number 4 bus stop here?

3 **IN CONVERSATION**: TAXI

2 minutes

Le Marché d'Aligre, s'il vous plaît.
luh marshay daleegruh, seel voo play

The Aligre Market, please.

Oui, sans problème, monsieur.
wee. soñ problem musyuh

Yes, no problem, sir.

Vous pouvez me déposer ici, s'il vous plaît?
voo poovay muh dayposay eesee, seel voo play

Can you drop me here, please?

4 USEFUL PHRASES

4 minutes

Learn these phrases, then test yourself, using the cover flap.

| I want a taxi to the Arc de Triomphe. | **Je veux un taxi pour l'Arc de Triomphe.**
juh vuh uh taksee poor lark duh treeoñf |

| Please wait for me. | **Attendez-moi s'il vous plaît.**
atonday-mwah seel voo play |

| How long is the journey? | **Le trajet dure combien de temps?**
luh trajay dyur koñbyañ duh toñ |

| How do you get to the museum? | **Comment aller au musée?**
komont allay oh moozay |

| When is the next bus to the station? | **Quand est le prochain bus pour la gare?**
koñ ay luh proshen boos poor lah gar |

Cultural tip Métro lines (**lignes**) in Paris are known by their number. The name of the last station on the line is used to indicate the direction of the train. Follow the signs to the relevant end station—for example, **direction Place d'Italie**. Look out for the beautiful art deco **Métropolitain** signs retained in a few stations.

6 SAY IT

2 minutes

Do you go near the railway station?

The fruit market, please.

When's the next coach to Calais?

5 IN CONVERSATION: BUS

2 minutes

Vous allez près du musée?
vooz allay pray doo moozay

Do you go near the museum?

Oui. Ça fait un euro quatre-vingt-dix.
wee. sah fay oon uroh katruh-vañ-dees

Yes. That's one euro, ninety.

Dites-moi quand on arrive, s'il vous plaît.
deet mwah koñ toñ areev, seel voo play

Tell me when we arrive, please.

1 WARM UP
1 minute

Say "**I have...**" (pp14–15).

Say "**my father**," "**my sister**," and "**my parents**" (pp16–17).

Say "**I'm going to Paris**" (pp40–41).

En route
ON THE ROAD

Be sure to familiarize yourself with the French rules of the road before driving in France. French **autoroutes** (*motorways*) are fast but expensive. They are toll (**péage**) roads in which you usually take a ticket as you join the motorway and pay according to the distance traveled as you leave it.

2 🔊 MATCH AND REPEAT

Match the numbered items to the list, then test yourself, using the cover flap.

❶ **le coffre**
luh kofrue

❷ **le pare-brise**
luh parbreez

❸ **la prise**
lah preez

❹ **la borne de recharge**
lah born duh resharjh

❺ **la portière**
lah portyair

❻ **le pneu**
luh pnuh

❼ **les phares** (m)
lay far

❽ **le câble de recharge**
luh cabluh duh resharjh

windshield ❷

charger ❸

trunk ❶

door ❺

tire ❻

headlights ❼

charging ❽ cable

Cultural tip At self-service stations, the pump shows the fuel being added and the money owed. At unmanned gas stations, you may need to authorize a card payment before the pump starts working. Electric cars can be charged at public charging stations, paid for by card or app, and could take up to half a day to fully charge.

3 🔊 ROAD SIGNS

Sens unique
sons ooneek
One-way

Rond-point
roñ pwañ
Roundabout

CÉDEZ LE PASSAGE

Cédez le passage
seday luh passarj
Give way

4 🔊 USEFUL PHRASES

2 minutes

Learn these phrases, then test yourself, using the cover flap.

My turn signal doesn't work. **Mon clignotant ne marche pas.**
moñ kleenyoe-toñ nuh marsh pah

Fill it up, please. **Le plein, s'il vous plaît.**
luh plañ, seel voo play

4 minutes

charging ❹ point/ station

5 🔊 WORDS TO REMEMBER

4 minutes

Familiarize yourself with these words, then test yourself, using the cover flap.

car	**la voiture**	*lah vwatyur*
gas	**l'essence** (f)	*laysans*
diesel	**le gazole**	*luh gazol*
oil	**l'huile** (f)	*lweel*
engine	**le moteur**	*luh motur*
transmission	**la boîte de vitesses**	*lah bwat duh veetess*
flat tire	**le pneu crevé**	*luh pnuh kruvay*
exhaust	**le pot d'échappement**	*luh poe dayshapmoñ*
driver's license	**le permis de conduire**	*luh pairmee duh kondweer*

6 SAY IT

2 minutes

My transmission doesn't work.

I have a flat tire.

2 minutes

Passage protégé
passarj protayjay
Priority road

Sens interdit
sons añtairdee
No entry

Défense de stationner
dayfoñs duh stahseeonay
No parking

Réponses *Answers*
(Cover with flap)

Révisez et répétez
REVIEW AND REPEAT

Transport

❶ **la voiture**
lah vwatyur

❷ **le taxi**
luh taksee

❸ **le bus**
luh boos

❹ **le train**
luh trañ

❺ **le vélo**
luh vayloe

❻ **le métro**
luh metroe

1 TRANSPORT

Name these forms of transport in French.

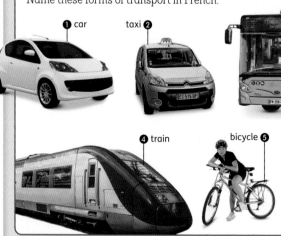

❶ car   taxi ❷

❹ train   bicycle ❺

Go and take

❶ **allons**
alloñ

❷ **vais**
vay

❸ **prend**
proñ

❹ **allez**
allay

❺ **prenez**
prunay

❻ **prends**
proñ

2 GO AND TAKE

4 minutes

Fill in the blanks with the correct form of **aller** (*to go*) or **prendre** (*to take*).

❶ **Nous** _____ **à la Tour Eiffel.** (aller)

❷ **Je** _____ **à la gare.** (aller)

❸ **Elle** _____ **rendez-vous lundi.** (prendre)

❹ **Où** _____-**vous?** (aller)

❺ **Que** _____ -**vous?** (prendre)

❻ **Je** _____ **le bœuf.** (prendre)

3 minutes

❸ bus

❻ metro

3 VOUS OR TU?

4 minutes

Use the correct form of *you*.

❶ You are in a café. Ask "Do you have croissants?"

❷ You are with a friend. Ask "Do you want a beer?"

❸ A businesswoman approaches you at your company reception. Ask "Do you have an appointment?"

❹ You are on the bus. Ask "Do you go near the station?"

❺ Ask your mother where she's going tomorrow.

❻ Ask your client "Are you free on Wednesday?"

Vous or tu?

❶ **Vous avez des croissants?**
voo zavay day krossoñ

❷ **Tu veux une bière?**
tew vuh oon biyair

❸ **Vous avez rendez-vous?**
voo zavay roñday voo

❹ **Vous allez près de la gare?**
voo zallay pray duh lah gar

❺ **Où vas-tu demain?**
oo vah-tew dumañ

❻ **Vous êtes libre mercredi?**
voo zet leebruh mairkrudee

4 TICKETS

4 minutes

You're buying tickets at a railway station. Join in the conversation, replying in French following the numbered English prompts.

Je peux vous aider?
❶ I'd like two tickets to Lille.

Aller-simple ou aller-retour?
❷ Return, please.

Voilà. Deux-cent-dix euros, s'il vous plaît.
❸ What time does the train leave?

À treize heures dix.
❹ What platform does the train leave from?

Quai numéro sept.
❺ Thank you. Goodbye.

Tickets

❶ **Je voudrais deux billets pour Lille.**
juh voodray duh beeyay poor leel

❷ **Aller-retour, s'il vous plaît.**
allay rutoor, seel voo play

❸ **À quelle heure part le train?**
ah kel ur par luh trañ

❹ **Le train part de quel quai?**
luh trañ par duh kel kay

❺ **Merci. Au revoir.**
mairsee. ovwar

En ville
ABOUT TOWN

1 WARM UP
1 minute

Ask "**How do you get to the museum?**" (pp42–43).

Say "**I want to take the metro**" and "**I don't want to take a taxi**" (pp40–41).

Most French towns still have a market day and a thriving community of small shops. Even small villages usually have a mayor and a town hall. There may be parking restrictions in the town center. Look out for signs for **parcmètres** (*pay and display*) and **défense de stationner** (*parking forbidden*).

2 ◀)) WORDS TO REMEMBER
4 minutes

Familiarize yourself with these words, then test yourself by using the cover flap.

la station service *la stasyoñ servees*	gas station
l'office de tourisme (m) *loffees duh torizmuh*	tourist office
le garage *luh gararj*	car repair shop
la piscine municipale *lah piseen mooneeseepal*	public swimming pool

town center **⑤**

church **⑥**

3 ◀)) MATCH AND REPEAT
4 minutes

Match the numbered locations to the list, then test yourself by using the cover flap.

❶ la mairie *lah mayree*

❷ le musée *luh moozay*

❸ le pont *luh poñ*

❹ la galerie d'art *lah galree dar*

❺ le centre ville *luh sontruh veel*

❻ l'église (f) *legleez*

❼ la place *lah plas*

❽ le parking *luh parking*

❶ town hall

❷ museum

❸ bridge

❹ art gallery

4 USEFUL PHRASES

4 minutes

Learn these phrases, then test yourself by using the cover flap.

Is there an art gallery in town?	**Il y a une galerie d'art en ville?** *eelyah oon galree dar oñ veel*
Is it far from here?	**C'est loin d'ici?** *say lwañ deesee*
There is a swimming pool near the bridge.	**Il y a une piscine près du pont.** *eelyah oon piseen pray doo poñ*
There isn't a library.	**Il n'y a pas de bibliothèque.** *eenyah pah duh bib-lee-yotek*

La cathédrale est en centre-ville.
lah kataydral et oñ sontruh veel
The cathedral is in the town centre.

5 PUT INTO PRACTICE

2 minutes

Complete this dialogue, then test yourself by using the cover flap.

Je peux vous aider?
juh puh voo zeday

Can I help you?

Ask: Is there a library in town?

Il y a une bibliothèque en ville?
eelyah oon bib-lee-yotek oñ veel

Non, mais il y a un musée.
noñ may eelyah uñ moozay

No, but there's a museum.

Ask: How do I get to the museum?

Comment aller au musée?
komont allay oh moozay

C'est là-bas.
say lah bah

It's over there.

Say: Thank you very much.

Merci beaucoup.
mairsee bohkoo

⑦ square

⑧ car park

WARM UP

1 minute

How do you say "**Near the station**"? (pp42–43).

Say "**Take the first on the left**" (pp40–41).

Ask "**Where are you going?**" (pp40–41).

Les directions
FINDING YOUR WAY

To help you find your way, you'll often find a **plan de la ville** (*town plan*) situated in the town, usually near the town hall or tourist office. In the older parts of French towns, there are often narrow streets in which you will usually find a one-way system in operation. Parking is usually restricted.

2 WORDS TO REMEMBER

Familiarize yourself with these words, then test yourself by using the cover flap.

les feux (m) *lay fuh*	traffic lights
la rue principale *lah roo prañseepal*	main road
le marché couvert *luh marshay coovair*	indoor market
la fontaine *lah fontayne*	fountain
la carte *lah kart*	map
les cartes en ligne (f) *lay kart oñ leenhyue*	online maps
traversez *travairsay*	cross over
le plan de la ville *luh plañ duh lah veel* town plan	

la rue *lah roo* street/road

le coin *luh kwañ* corner

Quartier du **Port** et de la **Vieille Ville**

la zone piétonne *lah zohn peeayton* pedestrian zone

3 IN CONVERSATION

Il y a un bon restaurant en ville?
eelyah uh boñ restoroñ oñ veel

Is there a good restaurant in town?

Oui, près de la gare.
wee, pray duh lah gar

Yes, near the station.

Et comment aller à la gare?
ay komont allay ah lah gar

And how do I get to the station?

5 SAY IT

2 minutes

Turn right at the end of the street.

It's across from the town hall.

It's ten minutes by bus.

4 minutes

| **la statue** |
| *lah statyoo* |
| statue |

4 USEFUL PHRASES

4 minutes

Learn these phrases, then test yourself by using the cover flap.

turn left/right	**tournez à gauche/droite**
	toornay ah gaush/dwrat
on the left/right	**sur la gauche/droite**
	sewr lah gaush/dwrat
first on the left	**la première à gauche**
	lah prumyair ah gaush
second on the right	**la deuxième à droite**
	lah duzyem ah dwrat
turn left at the main square	**tournez à gauche à la grande place**
	toornay ah gaush ah lah groñd plas
straight on	**tout droit**
	too dwrah
at the end	**au bout**
	oh boo
opposite	**en face de**
	oñ fass duh
How do I get to the swimming pool?	**Comment aller à la piscine?**
	komont allay ah lah piseen

Je me suis perdue.
juh muh swee pairdoo
I'm lost.

4 minutes

Tournez à gauche aux feux et puis tout droit.
toornay ah gaush oh fuh ay pwee too dwrah

Turn left at the traffic lights and then go straight.

C'est loin?
say lwañ

Is it far?

Non, à cinq minutes à pied.
noñ, ah sank minoot ah pyay

No, it's five minutes on foot.

Le tourisme
SIGHTSEEING

1 WARM UP
1 minute

Say "**Is there a museum in town?**" (pp48–49).

How do you say "**At six o'clock**"? (pp30–31).

Ask "**What time is it?**" (pp30–31).

Most national museums and art galleries close one day a week and on public holidays. Although shops are normally closed on Sundays, many will remain open all weekend in tourist areas. It is not unusual, particularly in provincial areas, for shops and public buildings to close at lunchtime.

2 **WORDS TO REMEMBER**

4 minutes

Familiarize yourself with these words, then test yourself, using the cover flap.

le guide *luh geed*	guide, guidebook, travel guide
le billet *luh beeyay*	entrance ticket
les heures d'ouverture (f) *lay zur doovairtyur*	opening times
le jour férié *luh joor fairiyay*	public holiday
l'entrée gratuite (f) *loñtray gratweet*	free entry

la visite guidée
lah viseet geeday
guided tour

Cultural tip The majority of public buildings and private offices close for public holidays, and many are also closed in August. If a public holiday falls on a Thursday, the French will often **faire le pont** (*make a bridge*)—in other words, take Friday off as well to make a long weekend.

3 **IN CONVERSATION**

Vous ouvrez cet après-midi?
voo zoovray set apray-meedee

Do you open this afternoon?

Oui, mais nous fermons à quatre heures.
wee, may noo fairmoñ ah katruh

Yes, but we close at four o'clock.

Vous avez un accès pour les fauteuils roulants?
voo zavay uñ aksay poor lay fohtuhee roolañ

Do you have wheelchair access?

4 USEFUL PHRASES

3 minutes

Learn these phrases, then test yourself, using the cover flap.

What time do you open/close?

Vous ouvrez/fermez à quelle heure?
voo zoovray/fairmay ah kel ur

Where are the toilets?

Où sont les toilettes?
oo soñ lay twalet

Is there wheelchair access?

Il y a un accès pour les fauteuils roulants?
eelyah uñ aksay poor lay fohtuhee roolañ

5 PUT INTO PRACTICE

4 minutes

Complete this dialogue, then test yourself using the cover flap.

Désolé. Le musée est fermé.
dezolay. luh moozay ay fairmay

Sorry. The museum is closed.

Ask: Do you open on Tuesdays?

Vous ouvrez le mardi?
voo zoovray luh mardee

Oui, mais nous fermons tôt.
wee, may noo fairmoñ toe

Yes, but we close early.

Ask: At what time?

À quelle heure?
ah kel ur

---

3 minutes

Oui, il y a un ascenseur là-bas.
wee, eelyah uñ asoñsur lah-bah

Yes, there's an elevator over there.

Merci, je voudrais quatre billets.
mairsee, juh voodray katruh beeyay

Thank you, I'd like four entrance tickets.

Voilà, et le guide est gratuit.
vwalah, ay luh geed ay gratwee

Here you are, and the guidebook is free.

1 **WARM UP**
1 minute

Say in French "**She is my stepmother**" (pp14–15).

What's the French for "**ticket**"? (pp38–39).

Say "**I am going to New York**" (pp40–41).

À l'aéroport
AT THE AIRPORT

Although the airport environment is largely international, it is sometimes useful to be able to ask your way around the terminal in French. It's a good idea to make sure you have a few one-euro coins when you arrive at the airport— you may need to pay for a luggage cart.

2 **WORDS TO REMEMBER**
4 minutes

l'enregistrement (m) — check-in
loñrejeestrumoñ

les départs (m) — departures
lay depar

les arrivées (f) — arrivals
lay zareevay

la douane — customs
lah doo-an

le contrôle des passeports — passport control
luh kontrol day passpor

le terminal — terminal
luh termee-nal

la porte d'embarquement — boarding gate
lah port doñbarkumoñ

le numéro de vol — flight number
luh noomairoe duh vol

Familiarize yourself with these words, then test yourself by using the cover flap.

Le vol 23 part du terminal 2.
luh vol 23 par doo termee-nal 2
Flight 23 leaves from Terminal 2.

3 **USEFUL PHRASES**
3 minutes

Learn these phrases, then test yourself by using the cover flap.

Le vol pour Nice est à l'heure?
luh vol poor nees et ah lur
Is the flight for Nice on time?

Le vol pour Londres est retardé.
luh vol poor londruh ay retarday
The flight to London is delayed.

Je ne trouve pas mes bagages.
juh nuh troov pah may bagarj
I can't find my baggage.

4 PUT INTO PRACTICE

3 minutes

Complete this dialogue, then test yourself by using the cover flap.

Bonsoir, monsieur. Je peux vous aider?
boñswar, musyuh. juh puh voo zayday

Good evening, sir. Can I help you?

Ask: Is the flight to Paris on time?

Le vol pour Paris est à l'heure?
luh vol poor paree et ah lur

Oui, monsieur.
wee musyuh

Yes, sir.

Ask: Which gate does it leave from?

Quelle est la porte d'embarquement?
kel ay lah port doñbarkumoñ

5 MATCH AND REPEAT

4 minutes

Match the numbered items to the list, then test yourself by using the cover flap.

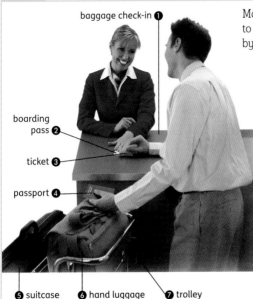

baggage check-in ❶

boarding pass ❷

ticket ❸

passport ❹

❺ suitcase   ❻ hand luggage   ❼ trolley

❶ **l'enregistrement des bagages** (m)
loñrejeestrumoñ day bagarj

❷ **la carte d'embarquement**
lah kart doñbarkumoñ

❸ **le billet**
luh beeyay

❹ **le passeport**
luh passpor

❺ **la valise**
lah valeez

❻ **le bagage à main**
luh bagarj ah mañ

❼ **le chariot**
luh shareeyoh

Réponses *Answers*
(Cover with flap)

Places

❶ **le musée**
luh moozay

❷ **la mairie**
lah mayree

❸ **le pont**
luh poñ

❹ **la galerie d'art**
lah galree dar

❺ **la cathédrale**
lah kataydral

❻ **le parking**
luh parking

❼ **la place**
lah plas

Révisez et répétez
REVIEW AND REPEAT

1 PLACES

4 minutes

Name these locations in French.

❶ **museum**   ❷ **town hall**   ❸ **bridge**

❹ **art gallery**

❺ **cathedral**

❻ **parking**   ❼ **square**

Car parts

❶ **le pare-brise**
luh parbreez

❷ **la prise**
lah preez

❸ **la borne de recharge**
lah born duh resharjh

❹ **la portière**
lah portyair

❺ **le pneu**
luh pnuh

❻ **le câble de recharge**
luh cabluh duh resharjh

2 CAR PARTS

Name these car parts in French.

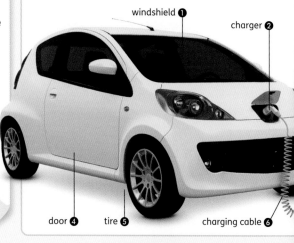

windshield ❶

charger ❷

door ❹   tire ❺   charging cable ❻

3 QUESTIONS

4 minutes

Ask the questions in French that match these answers.

❶ Le car part à huit heures.
luh kar par ah weet ur

❷ Le café, c'est deux euros cinquante.
luh kafay, say duh zuroh sankont

❸ Non, je ne veux pas de vin.
noñ. juh nuh vuh pah duh vañ

❹ Le train part du quai cinq.
luh trañ par doo kay sank

❺ Nous allons à Paris.
noo zalloñ ah paree

❻ Non, c'est cinq minutes à pied.
noñ, say sank minoot ah pyay

Réponses *Answers*
(Cover with flap)

Questions

❶ Le car part à quelle heure?
luh kar par ah kel ur

❷ C'est combien le café?
say koñbyañ luh kafay

❸ Vous voulez du vin?
voo voolay doo vañ

❹ Le train part de quel quai?
luh trañ par duh kel kay

❺ Où allez-vous?
oo allay voo

❻ C'est loin?
say lwañ

3 minutes

❸ charging point/ station

4 VERBS

4 minutes

Fill in the blanks with the correct form of the missing verbs.

❶ Je _____ anglais.

❷ Nous _____ le bus.

❸ Elle _____ à Paris.

❹ Il _____ trois filles.

❺ Tu _____ un thé?

❻ Combien d'enfants _____ -vous?

❼ Je _____ rendez-vous pour mardi.

❽ Où _____ les toilettes?

Verbs

❶ suis
swee

❷ prenons
prunoñ

❸ va
vah

❹ a
ah

❺ veux
vuh

❻ avez
avay

❼ prends
proñ

❽ sont
soñ

Réserver les chambres
BOOKING A ROOM

Ask in French "**Do you accept credit cards?**" (pp38–39).

Ask "**How much is that?**" (pp18–19).

Ask "**Do you have children?**" (pp12–13.)

There are different types of accommodations: **l'hôtel**, categorized from one to five stars; **la pension**, a small family-run hotel; and **les chambres d'hôte** (like bed and breakfast), often situated in beautiful old properties. Airbnb, offering accommodations in private rooms and homes, is also a popular option.

2 **USEFUL PHRASES**

3 minutes

Learn these phrases, then test yourself, using the cover flap.

Le petit-déjeuner est compris?
luh puhtee dayjunay ay koñpree

Is breakfast included?

Vous acceptez les animaux de compagnie?
voo zakseptay lay zanimoe duh koñpañee

Do you accept pets?

Vous avez un room service?
voo zavay uñ room survees

Do you have room service?

Il faut libérer la chambre à quelle heure?
eel foe leeburay lah shombruh ah kel ur

What time do I have to vacate the room?

3 **IN CONVERSATION**

Vous avez des chambres de libre?
voo zavay day shombruh duh leebruh

Do you have any rooms available?

Oui, une chambre double.
wee, oon shombruh doobluh

Yes, a double room.

Vous avez un lit d'enfant?
voo zavay uñ lee doñfoñ

Do you have a cot?

4 WORDS TO REMEMBER

4 minutes

Familiarize yourself with these words, then test yourself, using the cover flap.

La chambre donne sur le jardin?
lah shombruh don syur luh jardañ
Does the room have a view over the garden?

room	**la chambre** *lah shombruh*
single room	**la chambre simple** *lah shombruh sampluh*
double room	**la chambre double** *lah shombruh doobluh*
twin room	**la chambre twin** *lah shombruh twin*
bathroom	**la salle de bains** *lah sal duh bañ*
shower	**la douche** *lah doosh*
balcony	**le balcon** *luh balkoñ*
key	**la clé** *lah klay*
air-conditioning	**la climatisation** *lah kleematee-zasyoñ*
breakfast	**le petit-déjeuner** *luh puhtee dayjunay*

5 SAY IT

2 minutes

Do you have a single room?

Does the room have a balcony?

Cultural tip Chambres d'hôte are usually the only type of accommodations to include breakfast in the price of the room. In other types of hotels, you will usually be charged extra. Many two- or three-star hotels belong to the Logis de France association, which guarantees standards of accommodation and service.

5 minutes

Pas de problème. Combien de nuits?
pah duh prob-lem. koñbyañ duh nwee

No problem. How many nights?

Pour trois nuits.
poor trwah nwee

For three nights.

Très bien. Voici la clé.
tray byañ. vwasee lah klay

Very good. Here's the key.

WARM UP

1 minute

Ask "**Is there...?**" and say "**There isn't...**" (pp48–49).

What does "**Je peux vous aider?**" mean? (pp48–49).

Say "**They don't have any children**" (pp14–15).

À l'hôtel
IN THE HOTEL

Although the larger hotels almost always have bathrooms en suite, there are still some **pensions** and **chambres d'hôte** with shared facilities. This can also be the case in some economy hotels, where families can stay the night in low-cost, reasonably priced rooms.

2 **MATCH AND REPEAT**

6 minutes

Match the numbered items to the list, then test yourself, using the cover flap.

❶ **les rideaux** (m)
lay reedoe

❷ **le coussin**
luh koosañ

❸ **le canapé**
luh kanapay

❹ **la lampe**
lah lomp

❺ **l'oreiller** (m)
lorayay

❻ **le minibar**
luh meeneebar

❼ **le lit**
luh lee

❽ **la couverture**
lah coovurtyur

❾ **le dessus de lit**
luh dusoo duh lee

❿ **la table de chevet**
lah tabluh duh shuvay

❶ curtains ❷ cushion ❸ sofa ❹ lamp ❺ pillow

❻ minibar ❼ bed ❽ blanket bedspread ❾ bedside table ❿

Cultural tip When you arrive in your room, you may sometimes see a long sausage-shaped pillow on the bed called **le traversin**. Hard and not very comfortable, these are nowadays a largely decorative item. You can usually find soft rectangular pillows (**les oreillers**) in the cabinet. Do not hesitate to ask if you can't find any.

3 USEFUL PHRASES

5 minutes

Learn these phrases, then test yourself, using the cover flap.

The room is too cold/hot. **Il fait trop froid/chaud dans ma chambre.**
eel fay troe fwrar/shoh doñ mah shombruh

There are no towels. **Il n'y a pas de serviettes.**
eenyah pah duh survyet

I need some soap. **J'ai besoin de savon.**
jay buzwañ duh savoñ

The shower doesn't work very well. **La douche ne marche pas très bien.**
lah doosh nuh marsh pah tray byañ

The elevator has broken down. **L'ascenseur est en panne.**
lasohsur ay toñ pan

4 PUT INTO PRACTICE

3 minutes

Complete this dialogue, then test yourself, using the cover flap.

Je peux vous aider?
juh puh voo zayday

Can I help you?

Say: I need some pillows.

J'ai besoin d'oreillers.
jay buzwañ dorayay

Le personnel de chambre va les apporter.
luh pairsonnel duh shombruh vah lay zaportay

Housekeeping will bring some.

Say: And the television doesn't work.

Et la télévision ne marche pas.
ay lah telayveesyoñ nuh marsh pah

1 WARM UP
1 minute

Ask "**Can I?**" (pp34–35).

What is French for "**the shower**"? (pp60–61).

Say "**I need some towels**" (pp60–61).

Au camping
AT THE CAMPSITE

Camping is very popular in France, and the country has numerous well-organized campsites rated by a star system. Most towns have **un camping municipal** (*public campsite*), and there are also many private sites, including luxurious glamping sites. Campfires are usually forbidden, but you can often rent a grill.

2 USEFUL PHRASES

Learn these phrases, then test yourself, using the cover flap.

Je peux louer un vélo?
juh puh looway uñ vayloe
Can I rent a bicycle?

C'est de l'eau potable?
say duh loe potabluh
Is this drinking water?

Les feux de camp sont permis?
lay fuh duh koñ soñ pairmee
Are campfires allowed?

La musique forte est interdite.
lah moozeek fort ay añtairdeet
Loud music is forbidden.

Le camping est tranquille.
luh komping ay troñkeel
The campsite is quiet.

le branchement électrique
luh bronshmoñ aylektreek
electrical hook-up

le double toit
luh doobluh twah
fly sheet

la corde
lah kord
guy rope

le piquet
luh peekay
tent peg

3 IN CONVERSATION

J'ai besoin d'un emplacement pour trois nuits.
jay buzwañ d'uñ oñplasmoñ poor trwah nwee

I need a pitch for three nights.

Il y en a un près de la piscine.
eelyon ah uñ pray duh lah piseen

There's one near the swimming pool.

C'est combien pour une caravane?
say koñbyañ poor oon karavan

How much is it for a caravane?

5 SAY IT

2 minutes

I need a pitch for
four nights.

Can I rent a tent?

Where's the electrical
hook-up?

3 minutes

le bureau du camping
luh buroh doo komping
campsite office

la poubelle
lah poobel
trash can

les toilettes (f)
lay twalet
toilets

4 🔊 WORDS TO REMEMBER

4 minutes

Familiarize yourself with these words, then test
yourself, using the cover flap.

campsite	**le camping** *luh komping*
pitch	**l'emplacement** (m) *loñplasmoñ*
tent	**la tente** *lah tont*
ground sheet	**le tapis de sol** *luh tapee duh sol*
sleeping bag	**le sac de couchage** *luh sak duh koosharj*
air mattress	**le matelas pneumatique** *luh mataylah nyumateek*
caravan	**la caravane** *lah karavan*
camper van	**le camping-car** *luh komping-car*
camping gas	**le camping-gaz** *luh komping-gaz*
campfire	**le feu de camp** *luh fuh duh koñ*
drinking water	**l'eau potable** (f) *loe potabluh*
trash	**les détritus** (m) *lay daytreetoo*
showers	**les douches** (f) *lay doosh*

5 minutes

**Quatre-cent-cinquante
euros, avec une nuit
d'avance.**
*katruh soñ sankont uroh,
avek oon nwee davons*

Four hundred fifty
euros, one night
in advance.

**Je peux louer un
barbecue?**
*juh puh looway uñ
barbekyoo*

Can I rent a grill?

**Oui, mais vous devez
verser une caution.**
*wee, may voo duvay
vairsay oon kosiyon*

Yes, but you must pay
a deposit.

Les descriptions
DESCRIPTIONS

1 WARM UP
1 minute

Say "**hot**" and "**cold**" (pp60–61).

What is the French for "**room**" (pp58–59), "**bed**," and "**pillow**"? (pp60–61).

Adjectives are words used to describe people, things, and places. In French, you generally put the adjective after the thing it describes—for example, **une chambre froide** (*a cold room*). However, in some cases the adjective is placed before—for example, **un grand café** (*a large coffee*).

2 WORDS TO REMEMBER
7 minutes

Adjectives can change slightly, depending on whether the thing described is masculine (**le**), feminine (**la**), or plural (**les**), although the pronunciation often stays the same. Below, the masculine spelling is followed by the feminine. To form the plural, in most cases a silent "s" is added to the word, although some words take an "x" or "aux." Familiarize yourself with these words, then test yourself, using the cover flap.

grand/grande *groñ/groñd*	big/tall
petit/petite *puhtee/puhteet*	small
chaud/chaude *shoh/shohd*	hot
froid/froide *fwrah/fwrad*	cold
bon/bonne *boñ/bon*	good
mauvais/mauvaise *movay/movez*	bad
lent/lente *loñ/lont*	slow
rapide/rapide *rapeed/rapeed*	fast
bruyant/bruyante *breeyoñ/breeyont*	noisy
tranquille/tranquille *troñkeel/troñkeel*	quiet
dur/dure *dyuh/dyuh*	hard
mou/molle *moo/moll*	soft
beau/belle *boe/bell*	beautiful
laid/laide *leh/led*	ugly

la haute montagne *lah oht moñtanhyuh* high mountain

la basse colline *lah bas koleen* low hill

la vieille église *lah veeyay egleez* old church

la petite maison *lah puhteet mayzon* small house

Le village est très beau. *luh veelarj ay tray boe* The village is very beautiful.

3 USEFUL PHRASES

You can emphasize a description by using **très** (*very*), **trop** (*too*), or **plus** (*more*) before the adjective. Learn these phrases, then test yourself, using the cover flap.

This coffee is very hot. **Ce café est très chaud.**
suh kafay ay tray shoh

My room is very noisy. **Ma chambre est très bruyante.**
mah shombruh ay tray breeyont

My car is too small. **Ma voiture est trop petite.**
mah vwatyur ay troe puhteet

I need a softer bed. **J'ai besoin d'un lit plus mou.**
jay buzwañ d'uñ lee ploo moo

4 PUT INTO PRACTICE

Complete this dialogue, then test yourself, using the cover flap.

Voici la chambre. **La vue est très belle.**
vwasee lah shombruh *lah voo ay tray bell*

Here is the bedroom.

Say: The view is very beautiful.

La salle de bains est là-bas. **Elle est trop petite.**
luh sal duh bañ ay lah-bah *el ay troe puhteet*

The bathroom is over there.

Say: It is too small.

Nous n'avons pas d'autres chambres **Alors nous la prenons.**
noo navoñ pah dotruh shombruh *alor noo lah prunoñ*

We don't have any other rooms.

Say: Then we'll take it.

Révisez et répétez
REVIEW AND REPEAT

Adjectives

❶ chaude
shohd

❷ mou
moo

❸ bon
boñ

❹ petite
puhteet

❺ tranquille
troñkeel

1 ADJECTIVES

3 minutes

Fill in the blanks with the correct French masculine or feminine form of the adjective given in brackets.

❶ **La chambre est trop** _____ . (hot)

❷ **Je voudrais un oreiller plus** _____ . (soft)

❸ **Le café est** _____ . (good)

❹ **Cette salle de bains est trop** _____ . (small)

❺ **Vous avez une chambre plus** _____ ? (quiet)

Campsite

❶ le camping-car
luh komping-car

❷ la poubelle
lah poobel

❸ la tente
lah tont

❹ la corde
lah kord

❺ le branchement électrique
luh bronshmoñ aylektreek

❻ les toilettes
lay twalet

2 CAMPSITE

Name these campsite items in French.

camper van ❶   trash can ❷

❸ tent   guy rope ❹   ❺ electrical hook-up

3 AT THE HOTEL

4 minutes

You are booking a room in a hotel. Join in the conversation, replying in French following the numbered English prompts.

Je peux vous aider?
❶ Do you have any rooms free?

Oui, une chambre double.
❷ Do you accept pets?

Oui. C'est pour combien de nuits?
❸ Three nights.

Ça fait deux-cent-quarante euros.
❹ Is breakfast included?

Bien sûr, voici la clé.
❺ Thank you very much.

At the hotel

❶ **Vous avez des chambres de libres?**
voo zavay day shombruh duh leebruh

❷ **Vous acceptez les animaux de compagnie?**
voo zakseptay lay zanimoe duh koñpañee

❸ **Trois nuits.**
trwah nwee

❹ **Le petit-déjeuner est compris?**
luh puhtee dayjuhnay ay koñpree

❺ **Merci beaucoup.**
mairsee bohkoo

---

3 minutes

4 NEGATIVES

5 minutes

Make these sentences negative, using the correct form of the verb in brackets.

❶ **Je _____ d'enfants.** (avoir)

❷ **Elle _____ à Paris demain.** (aller)

❸ **Il _____ de vin.** (vouloir)

❹ **Je _____ le train pour Nice.** (prendre)

❺ **Le café _____ chaud.** (être)

❻ toilets

Negatives

❶ **n'ai pas**
nay pah

❷ **ne va pas**
nuh vah pah

❸ **ne veut pas**
nuh vuh pah

❹ **ne prends pas**
nuh proñ pah

❺ **n'est pas**
nay pah

1 WARM UP

1 minute

Ask **"How do I get to the station?"** (pp50–51).

Say **"Turn left at the traffic lights," "Cross over the street,"** and **"The station is opposite the café"** (pp50–51).

Les magasins
SHOPS

Small, traditional, specialized shops (**magasins**) are still common in French town centres, although you will see some chains as well. You can also find big supermarkets and shopping centres on the outskirts of major towns. Markets selling fresh local produce can be found everywhere. You can find out the market day at the tourist office.

2 MATCH AND REPEAT

Match the numbered shops to the list, then test yourself, using the cover flap.

❶ **la boulangerie**
  lah booloñjuree

❷ **la pâtisserie**
  lah pateesree

❸ **le tabac**
  luh tabah

❹ **la boucherie**
  lah boosheree

❺ **la charcuterie**
  lah sharkooterie

❻ **la librairie**
  lah leebrairee

❼ **la poissonnerie**
  lah pwasoñree

❽ **l'épicerie** (m)
  laypeesree

❾ **la banque**
  lah boñk

❶ baker

❷ cake shop

❹ butcher

❺ delicatessen

❼ fishmonger

❽ grocer

Cultural tip As well as supplying medicine and health products, a **pharmacie** (*pharmacy*) will sell expensive perfume and cosmetics plus everyday bars of soap and tubes of toothpaste. The latter can also be found at the supermarket or general store. The **tabac** (*tobacconist*) is the place for newspapers, magazines, postcards, and stamps but also has sweets, mobile phone top-ups, and souvenirs, and often incorporates a café and bar.

Où est le fleuriste?
oo ay luh flureest
Where is the florist?

Learn these phrases, then test yourself, using the cover flap.

Where is the hairdresser?	**Où est le coiffeur?** *oo ay luh kwafur*
Where do I pay?	**Je dois payer où?** *juh dwah payay oo*
I'm just looking, thank you.	**Je regarde, merci.** *juh rugard, mairsee*
Do you sell SIM cards?	**Vous vendez des cartes SIM?** *voo vonday day kart seem*
I'd like two of these.	**J'en veux deux.** *joñ vuh duh*
Can I place an order?	**Je peux passer une commande?** *juh puh passay oon komond*
Is there a department store in town?	**Il y a un grand magasin en ville?** *eelyah uñ groñ magazañ oñ veel*

4 minutes

❸ **tobacconist**

❻ **bookshop**

❾ **bank**

Familiarize yourself with these words, then test yourself, using the cover flap.

hardware shop	**la quincaillerie** *lah kañkayeree*
antiques shop	**l'antiquaire** (m) *lañteekair*
hairdresser	**le/la coiffeur(euse)** *luh/lah kwafur(urz)*
jeweler	**la bijouterie** *lah bee-jooteree*
post office	**la poste** *lah post*
shoemaker	**la cordonnerie** *lah kordoneree*
dry cleaner	**le pressing** *luh praysing*
confectioner	**le confiseur** *luh koñfeesur*
cheese shop	**la fromagerie** *lah fromajeree*

Where is the bank?
Do you sell cheese?
Where do I pay?

Au marché
AT THE MARKET

1 WARM UP
1 minute

What is French for "**40**", "**56**", "**77**", "**82**", and "**94**"? (pp30–31).

Say "**I'd like a big room**" (pp64–65).

Ask "**Do you have a small car?**" (pp64–65).

France uses the metric system of weights and measures. You need to ask for produce in kilograms and grams. You may find that the older generation still uses the term **une livre** (*a pound*), meaning half a kilogram. Some larger or more expensive items, such as melons or artichokes, may be sold **à la pièce** (*individually*).

2 🔊 MATCH AND REPEAT

Match the numbered items to the list, then test yourself, using the cover flap.

❶ **les poivrons** (m)
lay pwavroñ

❷ **les courgettes** (f)
lay korjet

❸ **la laitue**
lah laytyoo

❹ **les citrons** (m)
lay sitroñ

❺ **les tomates** (f)
lay toemat

❻ **les champignons** (m)
lay shoñpeeyoñ

❼ **les pommes de terre** (f)
lay pom duh tair

❽ **les avocats** (m)
lay zavokah

bell peppers ❶   zucchini ❷   lettuce ❸

❺ tomatoes   ❻ mushrooms   ❼ potatoes

3 🔊 IN CONVERSATION

Je voudrais des tomates.
juh voodray day toemat

I'd like some tomatoes.

Des grosses ou des petites?
day gros oo day puhteet

The large ones or the small ones?

Deux kilos de grosses, s'il vous plaît.
duh keeloe duh gros, seel voo play

Two kilos of the large ones, please.

5 SAY IT
2 minutes

Three kilos of bell peppers, please.

The mushrooms are too expensive.

How much is the lettuce?

4 ◀)) USEFUL PHRASES
5 minutes

Learn these phrases, then test yourself, using the cover flap.

Le fromage de chèvre est trop cher.
luh fromarj duh shevruh ay troe shair

The goat cheese is too expensive.

C'est combien ce fromage?
say koñbyañ suh fromarj

How much is that cheese?

Ce sera tout.
suh surah too

That'll be all.

Cultural tip France uses the common European currency, the euro. This is divided into 100 cents, which the French call **centimes** after the old divisions of the franc. You will usually hear the price given as: **dix euros vingt** (€10.20), **six euros soixante-treize** (€6.73), etc.

4 minutes

❹ lemons

❽ avocados

Et avec ceci, madame?
ay avek susee, ma-dam

Anything else, madam?

Ce sera tout, merci. C'est combien?
suh surah too, mairsee. say koñbyañ

That'll be all, thank you. How much?

3 minutes

Six euros cinquante.
sees uroh sankont

Six euros, fifty.

1 WARM UP
1 minute

What are these items you could buy in a supermarket? (pp22–23).

la viande
le poisson
le fromage
le jus de fruits
le vin
l'eau

Au supermarché
AT THE SUPERMARKET

Prices in supermarkets are usually lower than in smaller shops. They offer all kinds of products, with the larger **hypermarchés** (*superstores*) extending to clothes, household goods, garden furniture, DIY products, wine, full grocery lines, fresh produce, electronic items, and books. They may also stock regional products.

2 ◀))) MATCH AND REPEAT
5 minutes

Match the numbered items to the list, then test yourself, using the cover flap.

❶ **les produits d'entretien** (m)
lay prodwee doñtruh-tiañ

❷ **les produits de beauté** (m)
lay prodwee duh boetay

❸ **les fruits** (m)
lay froo-wee

❹ **les boissons** (m)
lay bwassoñ

❺ **les plats préparés** (m)
lay plah prayparay

❻ **les légumes** (m)
lay laygoom

❼ **les produits surgelés** (m)
lay prodwee surjulay

❽ **les produits laitiers** (m)
lay prodwee letyay

household products ❶
beauty products ❷
fruit ❸
drinks ❹
ready meals ❺
vegetables ❻
frozen foods ❼
dairy products ❽

Cultural tip For fruit and vegetables sold by the kilo, you will usually find a self-service weighing machine next to or near the produce. Alternatively, there may occasionally be a separate counter to weigh and price the produce.

3 USEFUL PHRASES

3 minutes

Learn these phrases, then test yourself, using the cover flap.

May I have a bag, please?	**Je peux avoir un sac, s'il vous plaît?** *juh puh avwar uñ sak, seel voo play*

Where is the drinks aisle?	**Où est le rayon des boissons?** *oo ay luh rayonn day bwassoñ*
Where is the checkout, please?	**Où est la caisse, s'il vous plaît?** *oo ay lah kes, seel voo play*

Please enter your PIN.	**Tapez votre code, s'il vous plaît.** *tapay votruh kod, seel voo play*

4 WORDS TO REMEMBER

4 minutes

Familiarize yourself with these words, then test yourself, using the cover flap.

milk	**le lait** *luh lay*
bread	**le pain** *luh pañ*
butter	**le beurre** *luh bur*
ham	**le jambon** *luh joñboñ*
salt	**le sel** *luh sel*
pepper	**le poivre** *luh pwavruh*
powdered soap	**la lessive** *lah leseev*
dishwashing liquid	**lle liquide vaisselle** *luh likeed vaysel*
toilet paper	**le papier toilette** *luh papyay twalet*
hand sanitizer	**le désinfectant pour les mains** *luh dayzuñfectoñ poor lay mañ*

5 SAY IT

2 minutes

Where is the dairy products aisle?

May I have some ham, please?

Where are the frozen foods?

Vêtements et chaussures
CLOTHES AND SHOES

1	**WARM UP**
	1 minute

Say "**I'd like...**" (pp24–25).

Ask "**Do you have...?**" (pp14–15)

Say "**38**," "**42**," and "**46**" (pp30–31).

Say "**large**," "**small**," "**bigger**," and "**smaller**" (pp64–65).

As in most of Europe, clothes and shoes in France are measured in metric sizes. Even allowing for conversion of sizes, French clothes tend to be cut smaller than American ones, and measurements may vary according to brand and style. Note that clothes size is **la taille**, but shoe size is **la pointure**.

2	**MATCH AND REPEAT**

Match the numbered items to the list, then test yourself, using the cover flap.

❶ **la chemise**
lah shumeez

❷ **la cravate**
lah kravat

❸ **la veste**
lah vest

❹ **la manche**
lah moñsh

❺ **la poche**
lah posh

❻ **le pantalon**
luh poñtaloñ

❼ **les chaussures** (f)
lay shohsyur

❽ **la jupe**
lah joop

❾ **les collants** (m)
lay kolloñ

shirt ❶
tie ❷
jacket ❸
sleeve ❹
pocket ❺
trousers ❻
shoes ❼
skirt ❽
tights ❾

Cultural tip Dress sizes usually range from 34 (US 2) through 46 (US 14) and shoe sizes from 35 (US 4) to 45 (US 11). For men's shirts, a size 41 is a 16-inch collar, 43 is a 17-inch collar, and 45 is an 18-inch collar.

3 ◀))) USEFUL PHRASES

5 minutes

Learn these phrases, then test yourself, using the cover flap.

Do you have a larger size? **Vous avez une taille plus grande?**
voo zavay oon tie ploo groñd

It's not what I want. **Ce n'est pas ce que je veux.**
suh nay pah sukuh juh vuh

3 minutes

I'll take the pink one. **Je prends la rose.** *juh proñ lah roz*

4 ◀))) WORDS TO REMEMBER

4 minutes

Colors are adjectives (pp64–65) and often have a masculine, feminine, and plural form. The feminine is usually formed by adding an **e** and the plural by adding an **s**. Familiarize yourself with these words, then test yourself, using the cover flap.

red	**rouge/rouge** *rooj/rooj*
white	**blanc/blanche** *bloñ/blonsh*
blue	**bleu/bleue** *bluh/bluh*
yellow	**jaune/jaune** *jon/jon*
green	**vert/verte** *vair/vairt*
black	**noir/noire** *nwar/nwar*

5 SAY IT

2 minutes

I'll take the yellow one.

Do you have this jacket in black?

I'd like a 38.

Do you have a smaller size?

Réponses *Answers*
(Cover with flap)

Révisez et répétez
REVIEW AND REPEAT

Market

❶ **les tomates**
lay toemat

❷ **les champignons**
lay shoñpeeyoñ

❸ **les courgettes**
lay korjet

❹ **les pommes de terre**
lay pom duh tair

❺ **les avocats**
lay zavokah

❻ **la laitue**
lah laytyoo

1 MARKET

3 minutes

Name these vegetables in French.

❶ tomatoes   ❸ zucchini   ❺ avocados

❷ mushrooms   ❹ potatoes   ❻ lettuce

Description

❶ These shoes are too expensive.

❷ My room is very small.

❸ I need a softer bed.

2 DESCRIPTION

2 minutes

What do these sentences mean?

❶ **Ces chaussures sont trop chères.**

❷ **Ma chambre est très petite.**

❸ **J'ai besoin d'un lit plus mou.**

Shops

❶ **la boulangerie**
lah booloñjuree

❷ **l'épicerie**
laypeesree

❸ **la librairie**
lah leebrairee

❹ **la poissonnerie**
lah pwasoñree

❺ **la pâtisserie**
lah pateesree

❻ **la boucherie**
lah boosheree

3 SHOPS

3 minutes

Name these shops in French.

❶ baker

❷ grocer

❸ bookshop

❹ fishmonger

❺ cake shop

❻ butcher

4 SUPERMARKET

3 minutes

Name these products in French.

❶ household products

❷ beauty products

❸ drinks

❹ dairy products

❺ frozen foods

Supermarket

❶ **les produits d'entretien**
lay prodwee doñtruh-tiañ

❷ **les produits de beauté**
lay prodwee duh boetay

❸ **les boissons**
lay bwassoñ

❹ **les produits laitiers**
lay prodwee letyay

❺ **les produits surgelés**
lay prodwee surjulay

5 MUSEUM

4 minutes

You are buying entrance tickets at a museum. Join in the conversation, replying in French following the numbered English prompts.

Bonjour. Je peux vous aider?
❶ Three adults and two children.

Ça fait quatre-vingt-cinq euros.
❷ That's very expensive!

Nous ne faisons pas de réductions pour les enfants.
❸ How much is an audio guide?

Cinq euros.
❹ Five tickets and five audio guides, please.

Cent-dix euros, s'il vous plaît.
❺ Here you are. Where are the toilets?

Là-bas.
❻ Thank you very much.

Museum

❶ **Trois adultes et deux enfants.**
trwah zadoolt ay duh zoñfoñ

❷ **C'est très cher!**
say tray shair

❸ **C'est combien pour un audioguide?**
say koñbyañ poor uñ odyohgeed

❹ **Cinq billets et cinq audioguides, s'il vous plaît.**
sank beeyay ay sank odyohgeed, seel voo play

❺ **Voilà. Où sont les toilettes?**
vwalah. oo soñ lay twalet

❻ **Merci beaucoup.**
mairsee bohkoo

1 WARM UP
1 minute

Ask **"Which platform?"** (pp38–39).

What is the French for these family members: **"sister"**, **"brother"**, **"son"**, **"daughter"**, **"mother"**, and **"father"**? (pp10–11).

Occupations
JOBS

Some occupations have a different form when the person is female—for example, **infirmier** (*male nurse*) and **infirmière** (*female nurse*). Others remain the same for men and women. When you state your occupation, you don't need to use **un/une** (*a*), as in: **je suis éditeur(trice)** (*I'm an editor*).

2 WORDS TO REMEMBER: JOBS
7 minutes

Familiarize yourself with these words, then test yourself, using the cover flap. The feminine form is given in brackets.

le médecin *luh medsañ*	doctor
le/la dentiste *luh/lah doñteest*	dentist
l'infirmier(ière) *lañfairmyay(yair)*	nurse
le/la professeur(e) *luh/lah profesur*	teacher
le/la comptable *luh/lah koñtabluh*	accountant
l'avocat(e) *lavokah(aht)*	lawyer
le/la designer *luh/lah deesienur*	designer
le/la consultant(e) *luh/lah koñsooltoñ(oñt)*	consultant
le/la secrétaire *luh/lah sekraytair*	secretary
le/la commerçant(e) *luh/lah komairsoñ(oñt)*	shopkeeper
l'électricien(ne) *laylektreesyañ(en)*	electrician
le/la plombier(ière) *luh/lah ploñbyay(yair)*	plumber
le/la cuisinier(ière) *luh/lah kweeseenay(yair)*	cook/chef
l'ingénieur(e) *lañjaynyur*	engineer
à mon compte *ah moñ kont*	self-employed

Je suis plombier.
juh swee ploñbyay
I'm a plumber.

Elle est professeure.
el ay profesur
She is a teacher.

3 PUT INTO PRACTICE

4 minutes

Complete this dialogue, then test yourself, using the cover flap.

Quelle est votre profession?
kel ay votruh profesyoñ

What do you do?

Say: I am a consultant.

Je suis consultant.
juh swee koñsooltoñ

Vous travaillez pour quelle compagnie?
voo trav-eyeyay poor kel koñpanee

What company do you work for?

Say: I'm self-employed.

Je suis à mon compte.
juh swee ah moñ kont

Comme c'est intéressant!
kom say añtayraysoñ

How interesting!

Ask: What is your profession?

Et quelle est votre profession?
ay kel ay votruh profesyoñ

Je suis dentiste.
juh swee doñteest

I'm a dentist.

Say: My sister is a dentist too.

Ma sœur est dentiste aussi.
mah sur ay doñteest ohsee

4 WORDS TO REMEMBER: WORKPLACE

3 minutes

Familiarize yourself with these words, then test yourself, using the cover flap.

head office	**le siège social** *luh syej sosyal*
branch	**la succursale** *lah sookoorsal*
department	**le département** *luh daypartumoñ*
reception	**la réception** *lah resepsyoñ*
manager	**le/la chef(fe)** *luh/lah shef*
trainee	**le/la stagiaire** *luh/lah stajyair*

Le siège social est à Lille.
lluh syej sosyal ay tah leel
The head office is in Lille.

Le bureau
THE OFFICE

<table>
<tr><td>

1   WARM UP
1 minute

Practice different ways of introducing yourself in different situations. Say your name, occupation, and any other information you'd like to give (pp8–9, pp14–15, and pp78–79).

</td><td>

An office environment or business situation has its own vocabulary in any language, but there are many items for which the terminology is virtually universal. Note that French computer keyboards have a different layout (AZERTY) than the standard English QWERTY convention.

</td></tr>
</table>

2 ◀))) WORDS TO REMEMBER
5 minutes

Familiarize yourself with these words, then test yourself, using the cover flap.

la réunion *lah rayoonyon*	meeting
le copieur *luh kopee-ur*	photocopier
l'ordinateur (m) *lordeenatur*	computer
le moniteur *luh moneetur*	monitor
la souris *lah sooree*	mouse
l'internet (m) *lañtairnet*	internet
l'email (m) *leemail*	email
le mot de passe *luh moh duh pas*	password
le code wifi *luh kod weefee*	Wi-Fi code
la conférence *lah konfayroñs*	conference
l'ordre du jour (m) *lordruh doo joor*	agenda
l'agenda (m) *lajeñdah*	diary
la carte de visite *lah kart duh veezeet*	business card
la messagerie téléphonique *lah mesah-juree telayfoneek*	voicemail

3 ◀))) MATCH

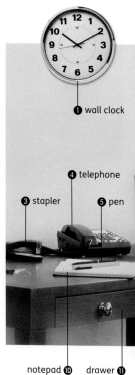

❶ wall clock

❹ telephone

❸ stapler   ❺ pen

notepad ❿   drawer ⓫

USEFUL PHRASES

4

2 minutes

Learn these phrases, then test yourself, using the cover flap.

| I want to send an email. | **Je veux envoyer un email.** |
| | *juh vuh oñvwayay uñ eemail* |

5 **SAY IT**

2 minutes

I'd like to arrange a conference.

Do you have a business card?

I have a laptop.

| I need to make some photocopies. | **J'ai besoin de faire des photocopies.** |
| | *jay buzwañ duh fair day fotokopee* |

| I'd like to arrange an appointment. | **Je voudrais prendre rendez-vous.** |
| | *juh voodray proñdruh roñday-voo* |

AND REPEAT

5 minutes

Match the numbered items to the list, then test yourself, using the cover flap.

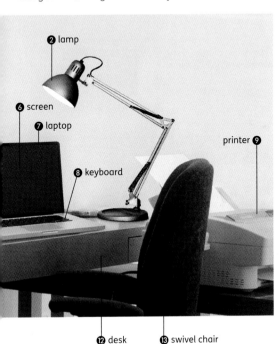

- ② lamp
- ⑥ screen
- ⑦ laptop
- printer ⑨
- ⑧ keyboard
- ⑫ desk
- ⑬ swivel chair

❶ **l'horloge murale** (f)
lorloj myural

❷ **la lampe**
lah lomp

❸ **l'agrafeuse** (f)
lagrafurz

❹ **le téléphone**
luh telayfon

❺ **le stylo**
luh steeloh

❻ **l'écran** (m)
laykroñ

❼ **l'ordinateur portable** (m)
lordeenatur portabluh

❽ **le clavier**
luh klaveeyay

❾ **l'imprimante** (f)
lampreemont

❿ **le bloc-notes**
luh blok-not

⓫ **le tiroir**
luh teerwar

⓬ **le bureau**
luh byuroh

⓭ **la chaise tournante**
lah shayz toornont

Le monde académique
ACADEMIC WORLD

Say "**How interesting!**" (pp78–79), "**library**" (pp48–49), and "**appointment**" (pp32–33).

Ask "**What is your profession?**"; answer "**I'm an engineer**" (pp78–79).

In France, as is now becoming standard across the EU, the first degree is **une licence** (*bachelor's*), followed by **un master** (*master's*) and then by **un doctorat** (*PhD*). Paris has several universities, often referred to by Roman numerals, such as Paris V.

---

2 **USEFUL PHRASES**

3 minutes

Learn these phrases, then test yourself, using the cover flap.

Quel est votre domaine?
kel ay votruh domayn

What is your field?

Je fais de la recherche en chimie.
juh fay duh lah reshairsh oñ sheemee

I am doing research in chemistry.

J'ai une licence en droit.
jay oon leesons oñ dwrah

I have a degree in law.

Je fais une présentation sur l'architecture moderne.
juh fay oon praysoñtasyoñ syur larsheetektur modairn

I am giving a presentation on modern architecture.

---

3 **IN CONVERSATION**

Bonjour, je suis le professeur Stein.
boñjoor, juh swee luh profesur stayeen

Hello, I'm Professor Stein.

De quelle université êtes-vous?
duh kel ooneevair-sitay et voo

Which university are you from?

Je suis déléguée de l'université Paris II.
juh swee daylaygay duh looneevair-sitay paree duh

I'm the delegate from Paris II University.

4 WORDS TO REMEMBER

4 minutes

Familiarize yourself with these words, then test yourself, using the cover flap.

Nous avons un stand à la foire.
noo zavon uñ stond ah lah fwar
We have a stand at the trade fair.

conference	**la conférence** *lah koñfayroñs*
trade fair	**la foire** *lah fwar*
seminar	**le séminaire** *luh semeenair*
lecture hall	**l'amphithéâtre** (m) *loñfeetayatruh*
conference room	**la salle de conférences** *lah sal duh koñfayroñs*
exhibition	**l'exposition** (f) *lekspohzeesyoñ*
library	**la bibliothèque** *lah biblee-yotek*
university lecturer	**le/la maître(resse) de conférences** *luh/lah metruh(ress) duh koñfayroñs*
professor	**le/la professeur(e)** *luh/lah profesur*
medicine	**la médecine** *lah medseen*
science	**la science** *lah siyons*
literature	**la littérature** *lah leetairatyur*
engineering	**l'ingénierie** (f) *lahjayneeuree*

5 SAY IT

2 minutes

I'm doing research in medicine.

I have a degree in literature.

She's the professor.

5 minutes

Quel est votre domaine?
kel ay votruh domayn

What's your field?

Je fais de la recherche en ingénierie.
juh fay duh lah reshairsh oñ lahjayneeuree

I'm doing research in engineering.

Comme c'est intéressant.
kom say añtayraysoñ

How interesting.

Les affaires
IN BUSINESS

1 WARM UP 1 minute

Say "**I'm a trainee**"
(pp78–79).

Say "**I want to send
an email**" (pp80–81).

Say "**I'd like to arrange
an appointment**"
(pp80–81).

While on business trips to France, you will make a good impression and receive a more friendly reception if you make the effort to begin meetings with a short introduction in French, even if your vocabulary is limited. After that, everyone will probably be happy to continue the meeting in English.

2 WORDS TO REMEMBER

Familiarize yourself with these words, then test yourself, using the cover flap.

le planning *luh planning*	schedule
la livraison *lah leevraysoñ*	delivery
le paiement *luh paymoñ*	payment
le budget *luh bujay*	budget
le prix *luh pree*	price
le document *luh dokoomoñ*	document
la facture *lah faktyur*	invoice
le devis *luh duhvees*	quotation
les bénéfices (m) *lay baynayfees*	profits
les ventes (f) *lay vont*	sales
les chiffres (m) *lay sheefruh*	figures

le cadre
luh kadruh
executive

On signe le contrat?
oñ seenuh luh koñtrah
Shall we sign the
contract?

le contrat
luh koñtrah
contract

Cultural tip In general, commercial dealings are formal, but a lunch with wine is still part of doing business in France. As a client you can expect to be taken out to a restaurant, and as a supplier, you should consider entertaining your customers.

3 🔊 USEFUL PHRASES

6 minutes

Note that when asking *what...?* you use **quel(s)** with masculine words but **quelle(s)** with feminine words. Learn these phrases, then test yourself, using the cover flap.

Envoyez-moi le contrat s'il vous plaît.
oñvwayay mwah luh koñtrah, seel voo play

Please send me the contract.

Nous sommes convenus d'un planning?
noo som koñvunoo duñ planning

Have we agreed on a schedule?

Quand pouvez-vous faire la livraison?
koñ poovay voo fair lah leevraysoñ

When can you make the delivery?

Quel est le budget?
kel ay luh bujay

What's the budget?

Vous pouvez m'envoyer la facture?
voo poovay moñvwayay lah faktyur

Can you send me the invoice?

---

6 minutes

le client
luh kleeyoñ
client

le rapport
luh rapor
report

4 SAY IT

2 minutes

Can you send me the quotation?

Have we agreed on a price?

What are the profits?

Réponses *Answers*
(Cover with flap)

Révisez et répétez
REVIEW AND REPEAT

At the office

❶ **l'horloge murale (f)**
lorloj myural

❷ **l'ordinateur portable**
lordeenatur portabluh

❸ **la lampe**
lah lomp

❹ **l'imprimante (f)**
lampreemont

❺ **l'agrafeuse**
lagrafurz

❻ **le stylo**
luh steeloh

❼ **le bloc-notes**
luh blok-not

❽ **le bureau**
luh byuroh

1 AT THE OFFICE

Name these items in French.

wall clock ❶   ❷ laptop   ❸ lamp

❺ stapler   pen ❻   ❼ notepad   ❽ desk

Jobs

❶ **médecin**
medsañ

❷ **plombier(ière)**
ploñbyay(yair)

❸ **commerçant(e)**
comairsoñ(oñt)

❹ **comptable**
koñtabluh

❺ **professeur(e)**
profesur

❻ **avocat(e)**
avokah(aht)

2 JOBS

3 minutes

Name these jobs in French.

❶ doctor
❷ plumber
❸ shopkeeper
❹ accountant
❺ teacher
❻ lawyer

Réponses *Answers*
(Cover with flap)

4 minutes

❹ printer

3 WORK

4 minutes

Answer these questions following the numbered English prompts.

Vous travaillez pour quelle compagnie?
❶ I work for myself.

De quelle université êtes-vous?
❷ I'm at the University of Bordeaux.

Quel est votre domaine?
❸ I'm doing medical research.

Nous sommes convenus d'un planning?
❹ Yes. Can you send me the budget?

Work

❶ **Je suis à mon compte.**
juh swee zah moñ koñt

❷ **Je suis de l'université de Bordeaux.**
juh swee duh looneevair-sitay duh bordoe

❸ **Je fais de la recherche en médecine.**
juh fay duh lah reshairsh oñ medseen

❹ **Oui. Vous pouvez m'envoyer le budget?**
wee. voo poovay moñvwayay lah bujay

4 HOW MUCH?

4 minutes

Answer these questions in French, using the amounts given in parentheses.

❶ C'est combien le café? (€2.50)
❷ C'est combien la chambre? (€80)
❸ C'est combien pour un kilo de tomates? (€3.25)
❹ C'est combien l'emplacement pour quatre jours? (€200)

How much?

❶ **C'est deux euros cinquante.**
say duh zuroh sankont

❷ **C'est quatre-vingts euros.**
say katruh-vañ uroh

❸ **C'est trois euros vingt-cinq**
say twrah zuroh vañ-sank

❹ **C'est deux-cents euros.**
say duh soñ uroh

1 WARM UP

1 minute

Say "**I'm allergic to nuts**" (pp22–23).

Say the verb "**avoir**" (*to have*) in all its forms (je, tu, il/elle, vous, nous, ils/elles) (pp14–15).

Le corps
THE BODY

The most common phrase for talking about aches and pains is **j'ai mal à…** Don't forget that when **à** is placed in front of **le**, it becomes **au**, and in front of **les**, it becomes **aux** (the **x** is silent). For example, **j'ai mal au dos** (*I have a backache*) and **j'ai mal aux oreilles** (*I have an earache*).

2 MATCH AND REPEAT: BODY

6 minutes

Match the numbered parts of the body to the list, then test yourself using the cover flap.

❶ **la main**
lah mañ

❷ **le coude**
luh kood

❸ **les cheveux** (m)
lay shuhvuh

❹ **la tête**
lah tet

❺ **le bras**
luh brah

❻ **le cou**
luh koo

❼ **l'épaule** (f)
laypoll

❽ **la poitrine**
lah pwatreen

❾ **l'estomac** (m)
lestomah

❿ **la jambe**
lah jomb

⓫ **le genou**
luh juhnoo

⓬ **le pied**
luh piyay

hand ❶
head ❹
❷ elbow
❸ hair
❺ arm
shoulder ❼
❻ neck
❽ chest
stomach ❾
leg ❿
knee ⓫
foot ⓬

3 ◀)) **MATCH AND REPEAT**: FACE

3 minutes

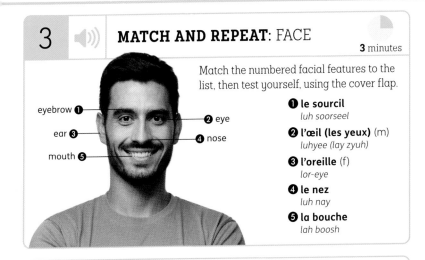

Match the numbered facial features to the list, then test yourself, using the cover flap.

eyebrow ❶
❷ eye
ear ❸
❹ nose
mouth ❺

❶ **le sourcil**
luh soorseel

❷ **l'œil (les yeux)** (m)
luhyee (lay zyuh)

❸ **l'oreille** (f)
lor-eye

❹ **le nez**
luh nay

❺ **la bouche**
lah boosh

4 ◀)) **USEFUL PHRASES**

3 minutes

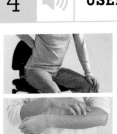

Learn these phrases, then test yourself using the cover flap.

I have a pain in my back.   **J'ai une douleur au dos.**
jay oon doolur oe doh

I have a rash on my arm.   **J'ai une rougeur au bras.**
jay oon roojur oe brah

I don't feel good.   **Je ne me sens pas bien.**
juh nuh muh soñ pah byañ

5 ◀)) **PUT INTO PRACTICE**

2 minutes

Complete this dialogue, then test yourself, using the cover flap.

Qu'est ce qui ne va pas?
keskee nuh vah pah
What's the matter?
Say: I don't feel good.

Je ne me sens pas bien.
juh nuh muh soñ pah byañ

Tu as mal où?
tew ah mal oo
Where does it hurt?
Say: I have a pain in my shoulder.

J'ai une douleur à l'épaule.
jay oon doolur ah laypoll

1 WARM UP
1 minute

Say "**I have a rash**" and "**I don't feel good**" (pp88–89).

Say the French for "**red**," "**green**," "**black**," and "**yellow**" (pp74–75).

À la pharmacie
AT THE PHARMACY

French pharmacists study for six to nine years before qualifying. They can give advice about minor health problems and are permitted to dispense a wide variety of medications, even giving injections if necessary. There is a **pharmacie de garde** (*24-hour duty pharmacy*) in most towns.

2 MATCH AND REPEAT
3 minutes

Match the numbered items to the list, then test yourself, using the cover flap.

❶ **le bandage**
luh boñdarj

❷ **le sirop**
luh seeroe

❸ **les gouttes** (f)
lay goot

❹ **la crème**
lah krem

❺ **le pansement**
luh poñsumoñ

❻ **la seringue**
lah surañg

❼ **le suppositoire**
luh soopozitwar

❽ **le cachet**
luh kashay

bandage ❶
drops ❸
adhesive ❺ bandage
syringe ❻
suppository ❼
syrup ❷
cream ❹
tablet ❽

3 IN CONVERSATION

Bonjour madame, vous désirez?
boñjoor, mad-dam. voo dayzeeray

Hello madam. What would you like?

J'ai mal à l'estomac.
jay mal ah lestomah

I have a stomachache.

Vous avez la diarrhée?
voo zavay lah dyaray

Do you have diarrhea?

4 WORDS TO REMEMBER

2 minutes

Familiarize yourself with these words, then test yourself, using the cover flap.

J'ai mal à la tête.
jay mal ah lah tet
I have a headache.

headache	**mal à la tête**	*mal ah lah tet*
stomachache	**mal à l'estomac**	*mal ah lestomah*
diarrhea	**la diarrhée**	*lah dyaray*
cold	**un rhume**	*uñ room*
cough	**une toux**	*oon too*
sunburn	**un coup de soleil**	*uñ koo duh sol-lay*
toothache	**mal aux dents**	*mal oh doñ*

5 USEFUL PHRASES

4 minutes

Learn these phrases, then test yourself, using the cover flap.

Do you have face masks? **Vous avez des masques?** *voo zavay day mask*

Do you have that as tablets? **Vous avez des cachets à la place?** *voo zavay day kashay ah lah plas*

I'm allergic to penicillin. **Je suis allergique à la pénicilline.** *juh swee zalurgeek ah lah peneesilin*

6 SAY IT

2 minutes

I have a cold.

Do you have that as a cream?

Do you have a cough?

---

3 minutes

Non, mais j'ai aussi mal à la tête.
noñ, may jay osee mal ah lah tet

No, but I also have a headache.

Prenez ça.
prunay sah

Take this.

Vous avez un sirop à la place?
voo zavay uh seeroe ah lah plas

Do you have that as a syrup?

Chez le docteur
AT THE DOCTOR

<table>
<tr><td>

1 WARM UP

1 minute

Say "**I need some tablets**" and "**He needs some cream**" (pp60–61 and pp90–91).

What is the French for "**I don't have a son**"? (pp14–15).

</td></tr>
</table>

In an emergency, dial 112 for an ambulance. If it isn't urgent, book an appointment with the doctor and pay when you leave. You can usually reclaim the money if you have comprehensive travel and medical insurance. You can find the names and addresses of local doctors at the town hall, tourist office, or pharmacy.

---

2 **USEFUL PHRASES YOU MAY HEAR**

3 minutes

Learn these phrases, then test yourself, using the cover flap.

Ce n'est pas sérieux.
suh nay pah seryuh
It's not serious.

Vous prenez des médicaments?
voo prunay day maydikamoñ
Are you taking any medications?

Vous avez une infection rénale.
voo zavay oon añfeksyoñ raynal
You have a kidney infection.

Vous avez besoin d'aller à l'hôpital.
voo zavay buzwañ dalay ah lopeetal
You need to go to the hospital.

Ouvrez la bouche, s'il vous plaît.
oovray lah boosh, seel voo play
Please open your mouth.

Vous avez besoin de tests.
voo zavay buzwañ duh test
You need to have tests.

---

3  **IN CONVERSATION**

Qu'est-ce qui ne va pas?
keskee nuh vah pah

What's the matter?

J'ai une douleur à la poitrine.
jay oon doolur ah lah pwatreen

I have a pain in my chest.

Laissez-moi vous examiner.
lessay-mwah voo zekzaminay

Let me examine you.

4 🔊 USEFUL PHRASES YOU MAY NEED TO SAY

4 minutes

Learn these phrases, then test yourself, using the cover flap.

Je suis enceinte.
juh swee zoñsant
I'm pregnant.

I'm diabetic.	**Je suis diabétique.** *juh swee diyabeteek*
I'm epileptic.	**Je suis épileptique.** *juh swee zepeelepteek*
I'm asthmatic.	**Je suis asthmatique.** *juh swee zasmateek*
I have a heart condition.	**J'ai un problème cardiaque.** *jay uñ prob-lem kardeeyak*
I feel faint.	**Je vais m'évanouir.** *juh vay mayvanooweer*
I have a fever.	**J'ai de la fièvre.** *jay duh lah fyevruh*
It's urgent.	**C'est urgent.** *say turjoñ*
I'm here for my vaccination.	**Je suis là pour me faire vacciner.** *juh swee lah poor muh fayr vakseenay*

Cultural tip EU nationals can get free emergency medical treatment in France with a European Health Insurance Card (EHIC) or E111 form. For UK nationals, the Global Health Insurance Card (GHIC) has replaced the EHIC. Travellers from all other countries should make sure they have comprehensive travel and medical insurance.

5 SAY IT

2 minutes

Do I need tests?

My son needs to go to the hospital.

It's not urgent.

5 minutes

C'est sérieux?
say seryuh

Is it serious?

Non, vous avez seulement une indigestion.
noñ, voo zavay surlmoñ oon añdeejestyoñ

No, you only have indigestion.

Quel soulagement!
kel soolarjemoñ

What a relief!

1 WARM UP

1 minute

Ask **"How long is the journey?"** (pp42–43)

Ask **"Do I need...?"** (pp92–93)

What is the French for **"mouth"** and **"head"**? (pp88–89).

À l'hôpital
AT THE HOSPITAL

The main hospitals in France are attached to universities and are known as **Centres Hospitaliers Universitaires (CHU)**. It is useful to know a few basic phrases relating to hospitals for use in an emergency or in case you need to visit a friend or colleague in the hospital.

2 🔊 USEFUL PHRASES

5 minutes

Learn these phrases, then test yourself, using the cover flap.

Quelles sont les heures de visite? *kel soñ lay zur duh vizeet*	What are the visiting hours?
Des boucles magnétiques sont disponibles? *day bookluh manyayteek soñ disponeebluh*	Is a hearing loop available?
Ça va prendre combien de temps? *sah vah prondruh koñbyañ duh toñ*	How long will it take?
Ça va faire mal? *sah vah fair mal*	Will it hurt?
Allongez-vous ici, s'il vous plaît. *aloñjay voo zeesee, seel voo play*	Please lie down here.
Vous ne devez pas manger. *voo nuh duvay pah moñjay*	You must not eat.
Ne bougez pas la tête. *nuh boojay pah lah tet*	Don't move your head.
Vous avez besoin d'une analyse de sang. *voo zavay buzwañ doon analeez duh soñ*	You need a blood test.

Où est la salle d'attente?
oo ay lah sal datont
Where is the waiting room?

l'intraveineuse (f)
lañtravaynurz
intravenous drip

Ça va mieux?
sah vah meeyuh
Are you feeling better?

3 WORDS TO REMEMBER

4 minutes

Familiarize yourself with these words, then test yourself, using the cover flap.

Votre radio est normale.
votruh radyoh ay normal
Your x-ray is normal.

emergency department	**le service des urgences** *luh survees day zurjoñs*
x-ray department	**le service de radiologie** *luh survees duh radyo-lojee*
children's ward	**le service de pédiatrie** *luh survees duh paydyah-tree*
operating room	**la salle d'opération** *lah sal dopairasyoñ*
waiting room	**la salle d'attente** *lah sal datont*
elevator	**l'ascenseur** (m) *lasoñsur*
stairs	**les escaliers** (m) *lay zeskalyay*

---

4 PUT INTO PRACTICE

3 minutes

Complete this dialogue, then test yourself using the cover flap.

Vous avez une infection.
voo zavay oon añfeksyoñ

You have an infection.

Ask: Do I need tests?

J'ai besoin de tests?
jay buzwañ duh test

Tout d'abord, vous avez besoin d'une analyse de sang.
too dabor, voo zavay buzwañ doon analees duh soñ

First, you will need a blood test.

Ask: Will it hurt?

Ça va faire mal?
sah vah fair mal

5 SAY IT

2 minutes

Does he need a blood test?

Where is the children's ward?

Do I need an x-ray?

Non, ne vous inquiétez pas.
noñ, nuh voo zañkyatay pah

No, don't worry.

Ask: How long will it take?

Ça va prendre combien de temps?
sah vah prondruh koñbyañ duh toñ

Réponses *Answers*
(Cover with flap)

The body

❶ **la tête**
lah tet

❷ **le bras**
luh brah

❸ **la poitrine**
lah pwatreen

❹ **l'estomac**
lestomah

❺ **la jambe**
lah jomb

❻ **le genou**
luh juhnoo

❼ **le pied**
luh piyay

On the phone

❶ **Je voudrais parler à Caroline Martin.**
juh voodray parlay ah karoleen martañ

❷ **[your name] de l'imprimerie Laporte.**
[your name] duh lahpreemuree laport

❸ **Je peux laisser un message?**
juh puh laysay uñ mesarj

❹ **C'est bon pour le rendez-vous lundi à onze heures.**
say boñ poor luh roñday-voo lañdee ah onz ur

❺ **Merci, au revoir.**
mairsee, ovwar

Révisez et répétez
REVIEW AND REPEAT

1 THE BODY

4 minutes

Name these body parts in French.

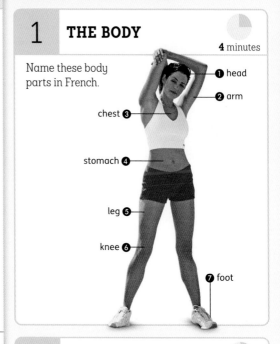

❶ head
❷ arm
chest ❸
stomach ❹
leg ❺
knee ❻
❼ foot

2 ON THE PHONE

4 minutes

You are arranging an appointment. Join in the conversation, replying in French following the numbered English prompts.

Allô, société Apex.
❶ I'd like to speak to Caroline Martin.

Oui, c'est de la part de qui?
❷ [your name] of Laporte printers.

Je suis désolée, la ligne est occupée.
❸ Can I leave a message?

Oui, bien sûr.
❹ The appointment on Monday at 11am is fine.

Très bien, au revoir.
❺ Thank you, goodbye.

3 CLOTHING

3 minutes

Name these items of clothing in French.

tie ❶

❷ jacket

❸ skirt

pants ❹

❺ tights

shoes ❻

4 AT THE DOCTOR'S

4 minutes

Say these sentences in French.

❶ I don't feel good.

❷ Do I need tests?

❸ I have a heart condition.

❹ Do I need to go to hospital?

❺ I'm pregnant.

❻ I'm here for my vaccination.

Réponses *Answers*
(Cover with flap)

Clothing

❶ **la cravate**
lah kravat

❷ **la veste**
lah vest

❸ **la jupe**
lah joop

❹ **le pantalon**
luh poñtaloñ

❺ **les collants**
lay kolloñ

❻ **les chaussures**
lay shohsyur

At the doctor's

❶ **Je ne me sens pas bien.**
juh nuh muh soñ pah byañ

❷ **J'ai besoin de tests?**
jay buzwañ duh test

❸ **J'ai un problème cardiaque.**
jay uñ prob-lem kardeeyak

❹ **J'ai besoin d'aller à l'hôpital?**
jay buzwañ dallay ah lopeetal

❺ **Je suis enceinte.**
juh swee zoñsant

❻ **Je suis là pour me faire vacciner.**
juh swee lah poor muh fayr vakseenay

Chez nous
AT HOME

WARM UP

1 minute

Say the months of the year in French (pp28–29).

Ask "**Is there an art gallery?**" (pp48–49) and "**How many brothers do you have?**" (pp14–15).

Many city dwellers live in apartment blocks (**les immeubles**), but in rural areas the houses tend to be detached (**individuelles**). If you ask "**combien de chambres?**", you will be told the number of bedrooms, whereas if you ask "**combien de pièces?**", the answer will include the number of bedrooms plus the living room, but not the kitchen or bathrooms.

2 🔊 MATCH AND REPEAT

Match the numbered items to the list, then test yourself, using the cover flap.

❶ **la gouttière**
lah gootyair

❷ **la cheminée**
lah shemnay

❸ **le toit**
lah twut

❹ **le volet**
luh volay

❺ **la fenêtre**
lah fenaytruh

❻ **la porte**
lah port

❼ **le mur**
luh myur

❽ **l'allée** (f)
lallay

❶ gutter ❷ chimney ❸ roof

❺ window ❻ door

Cultural tip Most French houses have shutters (**les volets**) at each window. These are closed at night and in the heat of the day. Curtains, where they are present, tend to be more for decoration. A single-story bungalow is known as **un pavillon**, and these are popular among the French as holiday homes in tourist resorts.

Quel est le loyer par mois?
kel ay luh lwayay par mwah?
What is the monthly rent?

5 minutes

❹ shutter

❼ wall ❽ driveway

3 🔊 USEFUL PHRASES
3 minutes

Learn these phrases, then test yourself, using the cover flap.

Il y a un garage?
eelyah uh gararj

Is there a garage?

C'est disponible quand?
say deesponeebluh koñ

When is it available?

C'est meublé?
say murblay

Is it furnished?

4 🔊 WORDS TO REMEMBER
4 minutes

Familiarize yourself with these words, then test yourself, using the cover flap.

room	**la pièce** *lah piyes*
floor	**le sol** *luh sol*
ceiling	**le plafond** *luh plafoñ*
basement	**la cave** *lah kav*
attic	**le grenier** *luh grunyay*
bedroom	**la chambre** *lah shombruh*
bathroom	**la salle de bains** *lah sal duh bañ*
living room	**le salon** *luh saloñ*
dining room	**la salle à manger** *lah sal ah moñjay*
kitchen	**la cuisine** *lah kwiseen*

5 SAY IT
2 minutes

Is there a dining room?

Is it large?

Is it available in July?

Dans la maison
IN THE HOUSE

<table>
<tr><td>

1

</td><td>

WARM UP

1 minute

</td></tr>
</table>

What is the French for "**room**" (pp58–59), "**desk**" (pp80–81), "**bed**" (pp60–61), and "**toilet(s)**" (pp52–53)?

How do you say "**soft**," "**beautiful**," and "**big**"? (pp64–65).

When you rent a house or villa in France, utilities such as electricity and gas may be included in the rent. However, generally you will be asked to pay for these separately, so be sure to check the lease agreement in advance. Additional charges might also extend to wood or other fuel for an open fire, which is usually charged by the cubic meter.

2 MATCH AND REPEAT

3 minutes

Match the numbered items to the list, then test yourself, using the cover flap.

❶ **le frigo**
luh freegoh

❷ **la cuisinière**
lah kwiseenyair

❸ **l'évier** (m)
levyay

❹ **le plan de travail**
luh plañ duh traveye

❺ **le micro-ondes**
luh meekro-ond

❻ **le four**
luh foor

❼ **la table**
lah tabluh

❽ **la chaise**
lah shez

fridge ❶   cooker ❷   sink ❸   ❹ counter

microwave ❺   oven ❻   table ❼   ❽ chair

3 IN CONVERSATION

C'est le four. *say luh foor* This is the oven.	**Il y a un lave-vaisselle aussi?** *eelyah uñ lav-vaysel osee* Is there a dishwasher as well?	**Oui, et il y a un grand congélateur.** *wee, ay eelyah uñ groñ koñjelatur* Yes, and there's a big freezer.

4 WORDS TO REMEMBER

2 minutes

Familiarize yourself with these words, then test yourself, using the cover flap.

Le canapé est neuf.
luh kanapay ay nurf
The sofa is new.

wardrobe	**l'armoire** (f) *larmwar*
armchair	**le fauteuil** *luh fohtuhee*
dresser	**la commode** *lah komohd*
fireplace	**la cheminée** *lah shemnay*
carpet	**le tapis** *luh tapee*
bathtub	**la baignoire** *lah bainwar*
bathroom sink	**le lavabo** *luh lavabo*
curtains	**les rideaux** (m) *lay ridoe*

5 USEFUL PHRASES

4 minutes

Learn these phrases, then test yourself, using the cover flap.

Is electricity included?	**L'électricité est incluse?** *laylektreesitay et añkloos*
I don't like the curtains.	**Je n'aime pas les rideaux.** *juh nem pah lay ridoe*
The carpet is old.	**Le tapis est vieux.** *luh tapee ay vyuh*

6 SAY IT

2 minutes

Is there a microwave?

I don't like the fireplace.

What a soft sofa!

---

3 minutes

L'évier est neuf?
levyay ay nurf

Is the sink new?

Bien sûr. Et voilà la machine à laver.
byañ syur. ay vwalah lah masheen ah lavay

Of course. And here's the washing machine.

Quel beau carrelage!
kel boe karlarj

What beautiful tiles!

Le jardin
THE GARDEN

1 WARM UP
1 minute

Say "**I need**" and "**you need**" (pp64–65, pp94–95).

What is the French for "**day**," "**week**," and "**month**"? (pp28–29).

Ask "**Is the wardrobe included?**" (pp100–101).

The yard of an apartment block may be communal, while houses generally have their own private yards. Check with the estate agent. In general, French yards are well-kept and reasonably formal, with hedges carefully trimmed and lawns regularly mowed. However, yards with a charming natural or "wild" look are also slowly gaining in popularity.

2 ◀)) WORDS TO REMEMBER
3 minutes

Familiarize yourself with these words, then test yourself, using the cover flap.

la tondeuse à gazon   lawn mower
lah toñdurz ah gazoñ

la fourche   fork
lah foorsh

la bêche   spade
lah besh

le râteau   rake
luh ratoe

la jardinerie   garden center
lah jardañree

3 ◀)) MATCH AND REPEAT

Match the numbered items to the list, then test yourself, using the cover flap.

tree ❶
lawn ❷
path ❸   weeds ❹   patio ❺

4 USEFUL PHRASES

4 minutes

Learn these phrases, then test yourself, using the cover flap.

Is the yard private?	**Le jardin est privé?** *luh jardañ ay preevay*
The gardener comes once a week.	**Le jardinier vient une fois par semaine.** *luh jardañyay vyañ oon fwah par suhmayn*
Can you mow the lawn?	**Vous pouvez tondre la pelouse?** *voo poovay toñdruh lah pelooz*
The garden needs to be watered.	**Le jardin a besoin d'eau.** *luh jardañ ah buzwañ doe*

5 SAY IT

2 minutes

The lawn needs to be watered.

Are there any flowers?

The gardener comes on Fridays.

5 minutes

- 6 hedge
- 7 flowers
- 8 flowerbed
- 9 plants
- 10 soil

❶ **l'arbre** (m)
larbruh

❷ **la pelouse**
lah pelooz

❸ **l'allée** (f)
lallay

❹ **les mauvaises herbes** (f)
lay movay zurb

❺ **la terrasse**
lah terass

❻ **la haie**
lah ay

❼ **les fleurs** (f)
lay flur

❽ **le parterre de fleurs**
luh partair duh flur

❾ **les plantes** (f)
lay ploñt

❿ **la terre**
lah tair

<table>
<tr><td>

1 WARM UP

1 minute

Say "**My name is John**" (pp8–9).

How do you say "**Don't worry**"? (pp94–95).

What is "**your**" in French? (pp12–13).

</td><td>

Les animaux
PETS

About two-thirds of all French households include at least one pet, who is often treated like a member of the family. Pet passports may be available to allow travelers to take their pets with them to France. Consult your vet for details of how to obtain the necessary vaccinations and paperwork.

</td></tr>
</table>

2 🔊 MATCH AND REPEAT

Match the numbered animals to the list, then test yourself, using the cover flap.

❶ **le lapin**
 luh lapañ

❷ **le poisson**
 luh pwassoñ

❸ **l'oiseau** (m)
 lwazoe

❹ **le chat**
 luh shah

❺ **le chien**
 luh shiañ

❻ **le hamster**
 luh amstair

❷ fish

❶ rabbit

dog ❺

❹ cat

3 🔊 USEFUL PHRASES

4 minutes

Learn these phrases, then test yourself, using the cover flap.

Ce chien est gentil?
suh shiañ ay joñtee
Is this dog friendly?

Je peux amener mon chien guide?
juh puh amunay moñ shiañ geed
Can I bring my guide dog?

J'ai peur des chats.
jay pur day shah
I'm frightened of cats.

Mon chien ne mord pas.
moñ shiañ nuh mor pah
My dog doesn't bite.

Ce chat est plein de puces.
suh shah ay plañ duh pous
This cat is full of fleas.

Cultural tip Many dogs in France are working or guard dogs, and you may encounter them tethered or roaming free. Approach farms and rural houses with care and keep away from the dog's territory. Look out for warning signs, such as **attention au chien** (*beware of the dog*).

3 minutes

bird **3**

hamster **6**

4 WORDS TO REMEMBER

4 minutes

Familiarize yourself with these words, then test yourself, using the cover flap.

vet	**le/la vétérinaire** *luh/lah vetairinair*
vaccination	**la vaccination** *lah vaksinasyoñ*
pet passport	**le passeport pour animaux** *luh passpor poor animoe*
basket	**le panier** *luh panyay*
cage	**la cage** *lah karj*
bowl	**la gamelle** *lah gamel*
collar	**le collier** *luh kolyay*
lead	**la laisse** *lah less*
fleas	**les puces** (f) *lay pous*

Mon chien est malade.
moñ shiañ ay malahd
My dog is not well.

5 PUT INTO PRACTICE

3 minutes

Complete this dialogue, then test yourself, using the cover flap.

C'est votre chien?
say votruh shiañ
Is this your dog?
Say: Yes, he's named Sandy.

Oui, il s'appelle Sandy.
wee, eel sapell Sandy

J'ai peur des chiens.
jay pur day shiañ
I'm frightened of dogs.
Say: Don't worry. He's friendly.

Ne vous inquiétez pas. Il est gentil.
nuh voo zañkyatay pah. eel ay joñtee

Réponses *Answers*
(Cover with flap)

Révisez et répétez
REVIEW AND REPEAT

Réponses *Answers*
(Cover with flap)

Colors

❶ **noir**
nwar

❷ **blanche**
blonsh

❸ **rouge**
rooj

❹ **verte**
vairt

❺ **jaunes**
jon

1 COLORS

4 minutes

Fill in the blanks with the correct French masculine or feminine form of the color given in brackets.

❶ Vous avez cette veste en _____ ? (black)
❷ Je prends la jupe _____ . (white)
❸ Vous avez cette robe en _____ ? (red)
❹ Non mais j'ai une _____ . (green)
❺ Vous avez des chaussettes _____ ? (yellow)

Kitchen

❶ **le frigo**
luh freegoh

❷ **la cuisinière**
lah kwiseenyair

❸ **le four**
luh foor

❹ **l'évier**
levyay

❺ **le micro-ondes**
luh meekro-ond

❻ **la table**
lah tabluh

❼ **la chaise**
lah shez

2 KITCHEN

Name these items in French.

fridge ❶   cooker ❷   ❸ oven   ❹ sink

❺ microwave   ❻ table

3 HOUSE

4 minutes

You are visiting a house in France. Join in the conversation, replying in French following the numbered English prompts.

Voilà le salon.
❶ What a lovely fireplace!

Oui, et il y a aussi une grande cuisine.
❷ How many bedrooms?

Il y a trois chambres.
❸ Do you have a garage?

Non, mais il y a un grand jardin.
❹ When is it available?

Juillet.
❺ What is the monthly rent?

House

❶ **Quelle belle cheminée!**
kel bel shemnay

❷ **Combien de chambres?**
koñbyañ duh shombruh

❸ **Vous avez un garage?**
voo zavay uñ gararj

❹ **C'est disponible quand?**
say deesponeebluh koñ

❺ **Quel est le loyer par mois?**
kel ay luh lwayay par mwah

---

4 minutes

4 AT HOME

3 minutes

Name these things in French.

❶ washing machine ❹ dining room
❷ sofa ❺ tree
❸ attic ❻ garden

❼ chair

At home

❶ **la machine à laver**
lah masheen ah lavay

❷ **le canapé**
luh kanapay

❸ **le grenier**
luh grunyay

❹ **la salle à manger**
lah sal ah moñjay

❺ **l'arbre**
larbruh

❻ **le jardin**
luh jardañ

Le bureau de change, la banque et la poste
BUREAU DE CHANGE, BANK, AND POST OFFICE

You can exchange one currency for another at a bureau de change. You can also get cash at a bank ATM but may be charged a fee. The post office also serves as a bank, usually with ATMs available outside the building. Stamps are sold at the post office as well as at **le tabac** (p68).

---

2 **WORDS TO REMEMBER**: MAIL

3 minutes

Familiarize yourself with these words, then test yourself, using the cover flap.

la boîte aux lettres — mailbox
lah bwat oh letruh

la carte postale — postcard
lah kart post-tal

le colis — package
luh kolee

par avion — air mail
par avyoñ

en recommandé — registered mail
oñ rukomoñday

le code postal — zip code
luh kod post-tal

le/la facteur(trice) — postal carrier
luh/lah faktur(trees)

C'est combien pour le Royaume-Uni?
say koñbyañ poor luh royom yunee
How much is it for the United Kingdom?

le timbre
luh tambruh
stamp

l'enveloppe (f)
loñvuhlop
envelope

---

3 **IN CONVERSATION**: BUREAU DE CHANGE

Je voudrais changer de l'argent.
juh voodray shoñjay duh larjoñ

I would like to change some money.

Que voulez-vous changer?
kuh voolay voo shoñjay

What would you like to exchange?

Je voudrais acheter des euros pour cinq-cents dollars.
juh voodray ashuhtay day zuroh poor sank soñ dollar

I would like to buy euros for five hundred dollars.

4 WORDS TO REMEMBER: BANK

2 minutes

Familiarize yourself with these words, then test yourself, using the cover flap.

la carte bancaire
lah kart boñkair
debit card

Comment je peux payer?
komon juh puh payay
How can I pay?

bank	**la banque** *lah boñk*
ATM/ cashpoint	**le distributeur automatique** *luh distreebootur otomateek*
PIN	**le code** *luh kod*
cash	**les espèces** (f) **/le liquide** *lay zespess/luh likeed*
bills	**les billets** (m) *lay beeyay*
credit card	**la carte** *lah kart*
contactless payment	**le paiement sans contact** *luh paymoñ soñ kontakt*

5 USEFUL PHRASES

4 minutes

Learn these phrases, then test yourself, using the cover flap.

I'd like to change some money.	**Je voudrais changer de l'argent.** *juh voodray shoñjay duh larjoñ*
What is the exchange rate?	**Quel est le taux de change?** *kel ay luh toe duh shoñj*
What would you like to exchange?	**Que voulez-vous changer?** *kuh voolay voo shoñjay*

6 SAY IT

2 minutes

I'd like a stamp for the United States.

Can I pay by credit card?

Do I need my PIN?

3 minutes

Bien sûr. Vous avez une pièce d'identité?
byañ syur. voo zavay oon piyes deedoñteetay

Of course. Do you have any identification?

Oui, voilà mon passeport.
wee, vwalah moñ passpor

Yes, here's my passport.

Merci, voilà vos euros.
mairsee, vwalah voe zuroh

Thank you, here are your euros.

1 WARM UP

1 minute

What's the French for "**It doesn't work**"? (pp60–61).

Say "**today**" and "**tomorrow**" in French (pp28–29).

Les services
SERVICES

You can combine the French words on these pages with the vocabulary you learned in week 10 to help you explain basic problems and arrange most repairs. When scheduling building work or a repair, it's a good idea to agree on the price and method of payment in advance.

2 WORDS TO REMEMBER:
SERVICES

4 minutes

Familiarize yourself with these words, then test yourself, using the cover flap. The feminine form is given in brackets.

le/la plombier(ière) *luh/lah ploñbyay(yair)*	plumber
l'électricien(ne) *laylektreesyañ(en)*	electrician
le/la garagiste *luh/lah gararjeest*	mechanic
le/la constructeur(trice) *luh/lah koñstruktur(trees)*	builder
le/la décorateur(trice) *luh/lah daykoratur(trees)*	decorator
le/la charpentier(ière) *luh/lah sharpañtyay(yair)*	carpenter
le/la maçon(ne) *luh/lah massoñ(en)*	bricklayer
l'employé(e) de ménage *lomployay duh maynarj*	cleaning staff

Je n'ai pas besoin d'un garagiste.
juh nay pah buzwañ duñ gararjeest
I don't need a mechanic.

3 IN CONVERSATION

La machine à laver est en panne.
lah masheen ah lavay ay toñ pan

The washing machine has broken down.

Oui, le tuyau est cassé.
wee luh tweeyoh ay kassay

Yes, the hose is broken.

Vous pouvez le réparer?
voo poovay luh rayparay

Can you repair it?

4 USEFUL PHRASES

3 minutes

Learn these phrases, then test yourself, using the cover flap.

Je peux faire réparer ça où?
juh puh fair rayparay sah oo
Where can I get this repaired?

| Please clean the bathroom. | **Nettoyez la salle de bain, s'il vous plaît.** *netwuhyay lah sal duh bañ seel voo play* |

Can you repair the boiler? | **Vous pouvez réparer la chaudière?** *voo poovay rayparay lah shodyair*

Do you know a good electrician? | **Vous connaissez un bon électricien?** *voo konessay uñ boñ aylektreesyañ*

5 PUT INTO PRACTICE

4 minutes

Complete this dialogue, then test yourself, using the cover flap.

Votre clôture est cassée.
votruh klotoor ay kassay

Your fence is broken.

Ask: Do you know a good builder?

Vous connaissez un bon constructeur?
voo konessay uh boñ koñstruktur

Oui, il y en a un dans le village.
wee, eelyonah uñ doñ luh villarj

Yes, there is one in the village.

Ask: Do you have his phone number?

Vous avez son numéro de téléphone?
voo zavay soñ noomairoe duh telayfon

3 minutes

Non, vous avez besoin d'un nouveau.
noñ. voo zavay buzwañ duñ noovoh

No, you need a new one.

Vous pouvez faire ça aujourd'hui?
voo poovay fair sah oh-joordwee

Can you do it today?

Non, je reviens demain.
non, juh ruvyañ dumañ

No, I'll come back tomorrow.

Venir
TO COME

<table>
<tr><td>

1

1 minute

Ask "**How do I get to the library?**" (pp48–49).

How do you say "**cleaning staff**"? (pp110–111).

Say "**It's 9:30**," "**10:45**," and "**12:00**" (pp10–11, pp30–31).

</td><td>

The verb **venir** (*to come*) is another important verb. Other useful verbs are made up of **venir** with a prefix, such as **prévenir** (*to prevent*), **devenir** (*to become*), and **revenir** (*to come back*). These can be formed in the same way as **venir** (below). Remember that **je viens** can mean either *I come* or *I am coming*.

</td></tr>
</table>

2 🔊 **VENIR**: TO COME

6 minutes

Practice **venir** (*to come*) and the sample sentences, then test yourself, using the cover flap.

je viens *juh vyañ*	I come
tu viens *tew vyañ*	you come (informal singular)
il/elle vient *eel/el vyañ*	he/she comes
nous venons *noo vunoñ*	we come
vous venez *voo vunay*	you come (formal singular or plural)
ils/elles viennent *eel/el vyen*	they come (m/f)

Je viens de New York. *juh vyañ duh noo york*	I come from New York.
Nous venons tous les mardis. *noo vunoñ too lay mardee*	We come every Tuesday.
Il vient de Chine. *eel vyañ duh sheen*	He comes from China.

Ils viennent par le train.
eel vyen par luh trañ
They come by train.

Conversational tip You can use the phrase **je viens de...** (literally *I come from...*) to talk about something you have just done or have recently completed. For example, **je viens de faire les courses** (*I have just been shopping*) or **je viens d'envoyer un email** (*I have just sent an email*). To say *just* in the sense of *only*, as in *I eat just a sandwich for lunch*, the French use **seulement**: **je mange seulement un sandwich pour déjeuner**.

3 USEFUL PHRASES

4 minutes

Learn these phrases, then test yourself, using the cover flap.

Je viens de me réveiller.
juh vyañ duh muh rayvay-yay
I have just woken up.

When can I come?	**Je peux venir quand?**
	juh puh vuneer koñ
Where does she come from?	**Elle vient d'où?**
	el vyañ doo
The cleaning staff come every Monday.	**Les employés de ménage vient tous les lundis.**
	lay zomployay duh maynarj vyañ too lay luñdee
Come with me. (informal/formal)	**Viens avec moi./ Venez avec moi.**
	vyañ avek mwah/ vunay avek mwah

4 PUT INTO PRACTICE

4 minutes

Complete this dialogue, then test yourself, using the cover flap.

Bonjour, salon de coiffure Christine.
boñjoor, saloñ duh kwafur Christine

Hello, this is Christine's hair salon.

Say: I'd like an appointment.

Je voudrais un rendez-vous.
juh voodray uñ roñday-voo

Vous voulez venir quand?
voo voolay vuneer koñ

When do you want to come?

Say: Can I come today?

Je peux venir aujourd'hui?
juh puh vuneer oh-joordwee

Oui bien sûr, à quelle heure?
wee byañ syur, ah kel ur

Yes of course, what time?

Say: At 10:30 am.

À dix heures et demie.
ah deez ur ay dumee

La police et le crime
POLICE AND CRIME

If you are the victim of a crime while in France, you should go to a police station to report it. In an emergency, you can dial 112. You may have to explain your complaint in French, so some basic vocabulary is useful. In the event of a burglary, the police will usually come to the house.

1 WARM UP — **1** minute

What's the French for "**big/tall**" and "**small/short**"? (pp64–65).

Say "**The room is big**" and "**The bed is small**" (pp64–65).

2 🔊 **WORDS TO REMEMBER:** CRIME — **4** minutes

Familiarize yourself with these words, then test yourself, using the cover flap.

J'ai besoin d'un avocat.
jay buzwañ duñ avokah
I need a lawyer.

le cambriolage *luh kañbryolarj*	burglary
le rapport de police *luh rapor duh polees*	police report
le/la voleur(euse) *luh/lah volur(urz)*	thief
la police *lah polees*	police
la déposition *lah daypoziyoñ*	statement
le/la témoin *luh/lah taymwañ*	witness
l'avocat(e) *lavokah(aht)*	lawyer

3 🔊 **USEFUL PHRASES** — **3** minutes

Learn these phrases, then test yourself, using the cover flap.

l'appareil-photo *lapareye foto* camera

le porte-monnaie *luh port mohnay* wallet

J'ai été cambriolé(e). *jay aytay kañbryolay*	I've been robbed.
Qu'est-ce qui a été volé? *keskee ah aytay volay*	What was stolen?
Vous avez vu qui a fait ça? *voo zavay voo kee ah fay sah*	Did you see who did it?
Ça s'est passé quand? *sah say passay koñ*	When did it happen?

4 WORDS TO REMEMBER: APPEARANCE

5 minutes

Familiarize yourself with these words, then test yourself, using the cover flap. Remember, some adjectives have a feminine form.

Elle a les cheveux longs et noirs.
el ah lay shuvuh loñ ay nwar
She has long black hair.

Il est chauve avec une barbe.
eel ay shohv avek oon barb
He is bald and has a beard.

man	**l'homme** (m) *lom*
woman	**la femme** *lah fam*
tall	**grand/grande** *groñ/groñd*
short	**petit/petite** *puhtee/puhteet*
young	**jeune** *juhn*
old	**vieux/vieille** *vyuh/vyay*
fat	**gros/grosse** *groe/gros*
thin	**mince** *mañs*
long/short hair	**les cheveux longs/courts** (m) *lay shuvuh loñ/koor*
glasses	**les lunettes** (f) *lay loonet*
beard	**la barbe** *lah barb*

5 PUT INTO PRACTICE

2 minutes

Complete this dialogue, then test yourself, using the cover flap.

Il ressemblait à quoi? *eel ruzoñblay ah kwah*
What did he look like?
Say: Short and fat.

Petit et gros. *puhtee ay groe*

Et les cheveux? *ay lay shuvuh*
And the hair?
Say: Long with a beard.

Longs avec une barbe. *loñ avek oon barb*

Cultural tip In France, there is a difference between **la gendarmerie** and **la police**. **La gendarmerie** operates in smaller towns, and **la police** in major cities. Their appearance and uniform are similar, and officers from both forces carry guns.

Révisez et répétez
REVIEW AND REPEAT

To come

❶ viens
vyañ

❷ vient
vyañ

❸ venons
vunoñ

❹ venez
vunay

❺ viennent
vyen

1 TO COME

3 minutes

Fill in the blanks with the correct form of
venir (*to come*).

❶ Je _____ à quatre heures.

❷ Le jardinier _____ une fois par semaine.

❸ Nous _____ pour déjeuner mardi.

❹ Vous _____ avec nous?

❺ Mes parents _____ par le train.

Bank and post

❶ le colis
luh kolee

❷ les cartes postales
lay kart post-tal

❸ les timbres
lay tambruh

❹ la carte bancaire
lah kart boñkair

2 BANK AND POST

4 minutes

Name these items in French.

❶ package

❷ postcards

debit card **❹**

❸ stamps

Réponses *Answers*
(Cover with flap)

3 APPEARANCE

4 minutes

What do these sentences mean?

❶ C'est un homme grand et mince.

❷ Elle a les cheveux courts et des lunettes.

❸ Je suis petite et j'ai les cheveux longs.

❹ Elle est vieille et grosse.

❺ Il a les yeux bleus et une barbe.

Appearance

❶ He's a tall, thin man.

❷ She has short hair and glasses.

❸ I'm short, and I have long hair.

❹ She is old and fat.

❺ He has blue eyes and a beard.

4 THE PHARMACY

4 minutes

You are asking a pharmacist for advice. Join in the conversation, replying in French following the numbered English prompts.

Bonjour. Je peux vous aider?
❶ I have a cough.

Et vous avez aussi un rhume?
❷ No, but I have a headache.

Prenez ces cachets.
❸ Do you have that as a syrup?

Bien sûr. Voilà.
❹ Thank you. How much is that?

Six euros.
❺ Here you are. Goodbye.

The pharmacy

❶ **J'ai une toux.**
jay oon too

❷ **Non, mais j'ai mal à la tête.**
noñ. may jay mal ah lah tet

❸ **Vous avez un sirop à la place?**
voo zavay uñ seeroe ah lah plas

❹ **Merci. C'est combien?**
mairsee. say koñbyañ

❺ **Voilà. Au revoir.**
vwalah. ovwar

Les loisirs
LEISURE TIME

What is the French for "**museum**" and "**art gallery**"? (pp48–49).

Say "**I don't like the curtains**" (pp100–101).

Ask "**Do you want…?**" informally (pp24–25).

The French pride themselves on their love of the arts, including opera and film, and it is also not unusual for them to count politics or philosophy among their interests. Be prepared for any of these topics to be the subject of conversation in social situations.

2 🔊 WORDS TO REMEMBER

Familiarize yourself with these words, then test yourself, using the cover flap.

le théâtre theater
luh tay-atruh

la musique music
lah moozeek

l'art (m) art
lar

le cinéma cinema
luh sinaymah

les jeux vidéos (m) video games
lay juh viday-oh

la boîte de nuit nightclub
lah bwat duh nwee

le sport sport
luh spor

le tourisme sightseeing
luh torizmuh

la galerie balcony
lah galuree

les spectateurs (m) audience
lay spektahtur

l'orchestre (m) stalls
lorkestruh

J'adore l'opéra! I adore opera!
jador lopayra

3 🔊 IN CONVERSATION

Salut, Olivia, tu veux jouer au tennis ce matin?
saloo oleevia, tew vuh jooay oh tennees suh mattañ

Hi, Olivia, do you want to play tennis this morning?

Non merci, je vais faire autre chose.
noñ mairsee, je vay fayr otruh shoz

No thank you, I have other plans.

Oh, tu vas faire quoi?
oh, tew va fayr kwah

Oh, what are you going to do?

5 SAY IT
2 minutes

I'm interested in music.
I prefer sports.
I don't like video games.
Shopping bores me!

4 minutes

4 USEFUL PHRASES
4 minutes

Learn these phrases, then test yourself, using the cover flap.

What are your (formal/informal) interests? — **Quels sont vos/tes intérêts?**
kel soñ voe/tay zañtayray

What do you (informal) plan to do this morning? — **Qu'est-ce que tu vas faire ce matin?**
keskuh tew vah fair suh mattañ

I like the theater. — **J'aime le théâtre.**
jem luh tay-atruh

I prefer film. — **Je préfère le cinéma.**
juh prayfair luh sinaymah

I'm interested in art. — **Je m'intéresse à l'art.**
juh mañtairess ah lar

I hate shopping. — **Je déteste le shopping.**
juh daytest luh shopping

That bores me. — **Ça m'ennuie.**
sah moñwee

J'aime les jeux vidéos.
jem lay juh viday-oh
I love video games.

4 minutes

Je vais faire du tourisme! Tu veux venir avec moi?
juh vay fair doo torizmuh. tew vuh vuneer avek mwah

I am going sightseeing! Do you want to join me?

Ça a l'air bien, mais je veux jouer au tennis.
sah ah layr biañ, may juh vuh jooay oh tenees

That sounds nice, but I want to play tennis.

Pas de problème, bon match!
pah de prob-lem, boñ match

No problem, enjoy your game!

<table>
<tr><td>

1

1 minute

Ask "**Do you** (formal) **want to play tennis?**" (pp118–119).

Say "**I like the theater**" and "**I prefer sightseeing**" (pp118–119).

Say "**That doesn't interest me**" (pp118–119).

</td><td>

Le sport et les passe-temps
SPORT AND HOBBIES

The verb **faire** (*to do* or *to make*) is a useful verb for talking about hobbies and is also used when describing the weather. **Faire** is followed by **du**, **de la**, or **de l'**, as in **je fais de la peinture** (*I paint*). You can also use the verb **jouer** (*to play*) when talking about playing sports and music.

</td></tr>
</table>

2 **WORDS TO REMEMBER**

4 minutes

Familiarize yourself with these words, then test yourself, using the cover flap.

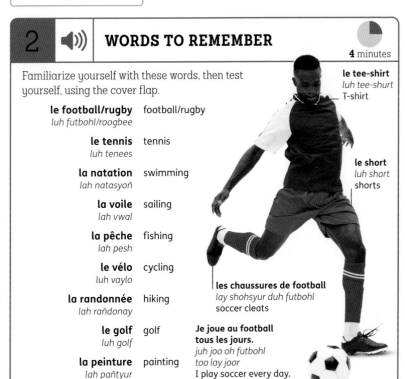

le football/rugby — football/rugby
luh futbohl/roogbee

le tennis — tennis
luh tenees

la natation — swimming
lah natasyoñ

la voile — sailing
lah vwal

la pêche — fishing
lah pesh

le vélo — cycling
luh vaylo

la randonnée — hiking
lah rañdonay

le golf — golf
luh golf

la peinture — painting
lah pañtyur

le tee-shirt
luh tee-shurt
T-shirt

le short
luh short
shorts

les chaussures de football
lay shohsyur duh futbohl
soccer cleats

Je joue au football tous les jours.
juh joo oh futbohl too lay joor
I play soccer every day.

3 **USEFUL PHRASES**

3 minutes

Learn these phrases, then test yourself, using the cover flap.

Je fais du rugby. — I play rugby.
juh fay doo roogbee

Il joue au tennis. — He plays tennis.
eel joo oh tenees

Elle fait de la peinture. — She paints.
el fay duh lah pañtyur

4 FAIRE: TO DO OR TO MAKE

 4 minutes

Practice **faire** (*to do* or *to make*) and the sample sentences, then test yourself, using the cover flap.

I do	**je fais** *juh fay*
you do (informal singular)	**tu fais** *tew fay*
he/she does	**il/elle fait** *eel/el fay*
we do	**nous faisons** *noo fayzon*
you do (formal singular or plural)	**vous faites** *voo fet*
they do (m/f)	**ils/elles font** *eel/el foñ*

Il fait beau pour faire de la randonnée aujourd'hui.
eel fay boe poor fair de lah rañdonay oh-joordwee
It's nice weather for hiking today.

What do you do?	**Que faites-vous?** *kuh fet voo*
I go hiking.	**Je fais de la randonnée.** *juh fay duh lah rañdonay*
We play tennis.	**Nous faisons du tennis.** *noo fayzon doo tenees*

5 PUT INTO PRACTICE

 3 minutes

Complete this dialogue, then test yourself, using the cover flap.

Qu'est-ce que vous aimez faire?
keskuh voo zemay fair
What do you like doing?
Say: I like playing tennis.

J'aime jouer au tennis.
jem jooway oh tenees

Tu fais du football aussi?
tew fay doo futbohl ohsee
Do you play soccer as well?
Say: No. I play rugby.

Non, je fais du rugby.
noñ, juh fay doo roogbee

Cultural tip France boasts a huge variety of regional games, such as pelota in the Basque country. The most popular of all is **pétanque** or **boules** (the French version of bocce), which is played in almost every town and village.

1 | WARM UP
1 minute

Say "**my husband**" and "**my wife**" (pp10–11).

How do you say "**lunch**" and "**dinner**" in French? (pp20–21).

Say "**Sorry, I'm busy**" (pp32–33).

Voir des gens
SOCIALIZING

The dinner table is the center of the French social world, and you can expect to do a lot of your socializing while enjoying good food and wine. It is best to use the more polite **vous** form to talk to people you meet socially until they call you **tu**, at which point you can reciprocate.

2 USEFUL PHRASES

Learn these phrases, then test yourself, using the cover flap.

Je voudrais vous inviter à dîner.
juh voodray voo zañveetay ah deenay
I'd like to invite you for dinner.

Vous êtes libre mercredi prochain?
voo zet leebruh mairkrudee prochen
Are you free next Wednesday?

Une autre fois peut-être.
oon awtruh fwah putetruh
Another time perhaps.

Merci de nous avoir invités.
mairsee duh noo zavwar añveetay
Thank you for inviting us.

l'hôtesse (f)
lohtess
hostess

3 IN CONVERSATION

Vous voulez venir dîner mardi?
voo voolay vuneer deenay mardee

Would you like to come to dinner on Tuesday?

Je suis désolée, je suis occupée.
juh swee dayzolay, juh swee zokoopay

I'm sorry, I'm busy.

Pourquoi pas jeudi?
poorkwah pah jurdee

What about Thursday?

Cultural tip When you visit someone for the first time, it is usual to take flowers or wine. Having seen their house, you can take a slightly more personal gift if invited again.

4 minutes

l'invité (f)
lanveetay
guest

4 WORDS TO REMEMBER

3 minutes

Familiarize yourself with these words, then test yourself, using the cover flap.

party	**la soirée** *lah swaray*
dinner party	**le dîner** *luh deenay*
cocktail party	**le cocktail** *luh koktail*
reception	**la réception** *lah raysepsyoñ*
invitation	**l'invitation** *lañveetasyoñ*

5 PUT INTO PRACTICE

3 minutes

Complete this dialogue, then test yourself, using the cover flap.

Vous pouvez venir à une réception ce soir?
voo poovay vuneer ah oon raysepsyoñ suh swah

Can you come to a reception this evening?

Say: Yes, I'd love to.

Oui, avec plaisir.
wee, avek playzeer

Ça commence à huit heures.
sah komoñs ah weet ur

It starts at eight o'clock.

Ask: Should I dress formally?

Il faut s'habiller?
eel foe sabeeyay

4 minutes

Avec plaisir.
avek playzeer

With pleasure.

Venez avec votre mari.
vunay avek votruh maree

Please bring your husband.

Merci. À quelle heure?
mairsee. ah kel ur

Thank you. At what time?

Révisez et répétez
REVIEW AND REPEAT

Animals

❶ le chat
luh shah

❷ le hamster
luh amstair

❸ le poisson
luh pwassoñ

❹ l'oiseau
lwazoe

❺ le lapin
luh lapañ

❻ le chien
luh shiañ

I like…

❶ Je joue au rugby.
juh joo oh roogbee

**❷ J'aime jouer
aux boules.**
jem jooway oh bool

**❸ Je n'aime pas
le football.**
juh nem pah luh futbohl

**❹ J'aime faire de
la peinture.**
jem fair duh lah pañtyur

---

1 ANIMALS

Name these animals in French.

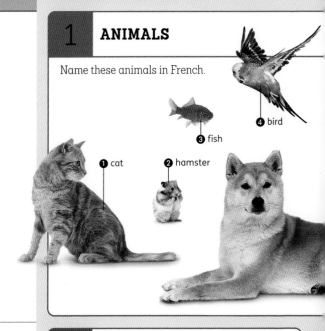

❹ bird

❸ fish

❶ cat

❷ hamster

---

2 I LIKE…

4 minutes

Say these sentences in French.

❶ I play rugby.
❷ I like playing bocce.
❸ I don't like soccer.
❹ I like painting.

❶

❷

❸

❹

3 minutes

5 rabbit

6 dog

---

3 TO DO

4 minutes

Fill in the blanks with the correct form of **faire** (*to do* or *to make*).

1 Tu _____ de la pêche?

2 Elle _____ de la voile.

3 Que _____-vous?

4 Il _____ froid aujourd'hui.

5 Vous _____ de la randonnée?

6 J'aime _____ de la natation.

To do

1 fais
fay

2 fait
fay

3 faites
fet

4 fait
fay

5 faites
fet

6 faire
fair

---

4 AN INVITATION

4 minutes

You are invited for dinner. Join in the conversation, replying in French following the numbered English prompts.

Vous voulez venir pour déjeuner vendredi?
1 I'm sorry, I'm busy.

Pourquoi pas samedi?
2 With pleasure.

Venez avec vos enfants.
3 Thank you. At what time?

À douze heures trente.
4 That's good for me.

An invitation

1 Je suis désolé(e), je suis occupé(e).
juh swee dayzolay, juh swee zokoopay

2 Avec plaisir.
avek playzeer

3 Merci. À quelle heure?
mairsee, ah kel ur

4 C'est bon pour moi.
say boñ poor mwah

Reinforce and progress

Regular practice is the key to maintaining and advancing your language skills. In this section, you will find a variety of suggestions for reinforcing and extending your knowledge of French. Many involve returning to exercises in the book and extending their scope by using the dictionaries. Go back through the lessons in a different order, mix and match activities to make up your own daily 15-minute program, or focus on topics that are of particular relevance to your current needs.

1 **WARM UP**
1 minute

Say "**He is**" and "**They are**" (pp14–15).

Say "**He is not**" and "**They are not**" (pp14–15).

What is French for "**the children**"? (pp10–11).

Match, repeat, and extend
Remind yourself of words related to specific topics by returning to the Match and Repeat and Words to Remember exercises. Test yourself, using the cover flap. Discover new words in that area by referring to the dictionary and menu guide.

Keep warmed up
Revisit the Warm Up boxes to remind yourself of key words and phrases. Make sure that you work your way through all of them on a regular basis.

2 🔊 **MATCH AND REPEAT**
5 minutes

Match the numbered items to the list, then test yourself, using the cover flap.

❶ **la gouttière**
lah gootyair

❷ **la cheminée**
lah shemnay

❸ **le toit**
lah twut

❹ **le volet**
luh volay

❺ **la fenêtre**
lah fenaytruh

❻ **la porte**
lah port

❼ **le mur**
luh myur

❽ **l'allée** (f)
lallay

❶ gutter ❷ chimney ❸ roof ❹ shutter

❺ window ❻ door ❼ wall ❽ driveway

Carry on conversing
Reread the In Conversation panels. Say both parts of the conversation, paying attention to the pronunciation. Where possible, try incorporating new words from the dictionary.

3 🔊 **IN CONVERSATION**

Salut, Olivia, tu veux jouer au tennis ce matin?
saloo oleevia, tew vuh jooay oh tennees suh mattañ

Hi, Olivia, do you want to play tennis this morning?

Non merci, je vais faire autre chose.
noñ mairsee, je vay fayr otruh shoz

No thank you, I have other plans.

Oh, tu vas faire quoi?
oh, tew va fayr kwah

Oh, what are you going to do?

Practice words and phrases
Return to the Words to Remember, Useful Phrases, and Put into Practice exercises. Test yourself, using the cover flap. When you are confident, devise your own versions of the phrases, using new words from the dictionary.

4 🔊 **USEFUL PHRASES**: MONTHS

2 minutes

Learn these phrases, then test yourself, using the cover flap.

My children are on vacation in August.	**Mes enfants sont en vacances en août.**
	may zoñfoñ soñ toñ vakons oñ oot

My birthday is in June.	**Mon anniversaire est en juin.**
	moñ naneevairsair ay toñ jwañ

5 **SAY IT**
2 minutes

I'm doing research in medicine.

I have a degree in literature.

She's the professor.

Say it again
The Say It exercises are a useful instant reminder for each lesson. Practice these with your own vocabulary variations from the dictionary or elsewhere in the lesson.

6 **BE OR HAVE**
5 minutes

Fill in the blanks with the correct form of **avoir** (*to have*) or **être** (*to be*).

❶ Je _____ anglaise.
❷ Nous _____ quatre enfants.
❸ Elle _____ une belle-fille.
❹ Nous _____ français.
❺ Vous _____ rendez-vous?
❻ Il n' _____ pas fatigué.
❼ Je n' _____ pas de portable.
❽ Nous _____ mariés.

Review and repeat again
Work through a Review and Repeat lesson as a way of reinforcing words and phrases presented in the course. Return to the main lesson for any topic about which you are no longer confident.

Using other resources

As well as working with this book, try the following language extension ideas:

Visit a French-speaking country and try out your new skills with native speakers. Find out whether there is a French community near you. There may be shops, cafés, restaurants, and clubs. Try to visit some of these and use your French to order food and drink and strike up conversations. Most native speakers will be happy to speak French with you.

Join a language class or club. There are usually evening and day classes available at a variety of different levels. Or you could start a club yourself if you have friends who are also interested in keeping up their French.

Look at French magazines and newspapers. The pictures will help you understand the text. Advertisements are also a useful way of expanding your vocabulary.

Use the Internet, where you can find all kinds of websites for learning languages, some of which offer free online help and activities. You can also find French websites for everything from renting a house to shampooing your pet. You can even access French radio and TV stations online. Start by going to a search engine and typing in a subject that interests you, or give yourself a challenge, such as finding a two-bedroom house for rent by the sea in Normandy.

Menu guide

This guide lists the most common terms you may encounter on French menus or when shopping for food. If you can't find an exact phrase, try looking up its component parts.

A

abats *offal*
abricot *apricot*
à emporter *to take away*
agneau *lamb*
aiguillette de bœuf *slices of rump steak*
ail *garlic*
aïoli *garlic mayonnaise*
à la broche *spit roast*
à la jardinière *with assorted vegetables*
à la normande *in cream sauce*
à la provençale *with tomatoes, garlic, and herbs*
à la vapeur *steamed*
amande *almond*
ananas *pineapple*
anchois *anchovies*
andouillette *intestine sausage*
anguille *eel*
à point *medium*
artichaut *artichoke*
asperge *asparagus*
assiette anglaise *selection of cold meats*
au gratin *baked in a milk, cream, and cheese sauce*
au vin blanc *in white wine*
avocat *avocado*

B

banane *banana*
barbue *brill (fish)*
bavaroise *light mousse*
béarnaise *béarnaise sauce*
bécasse *woodcock*
béchamel *white sauce*
beignet *fritter, doughnut*
beignet aux pommes *apple fritter*
betterave *beetroot*
beurre *butter*
beurre d'anchois *anchovy paste*
beurre noir *dark, melted butter*
bien cuit *well done*
bière *beer*
bière à la pression *draft beer*
bière blonde *lager*
bière brune *bitter beer*
bière panachée *shandy*

bifteck *steak*
bisque d'écrevisses *crayfish soup*
bisque de homard *lobster soup*
biscuit de Savoie *sponge cake*
blanquette de veau *veal stew*
bleu *very rare*
bleu d'Auvergne *blue cheese from Auvergne*
bœuf bourguignon *beef cooked in red wine*
bœuf braisé *braised beef*
bœuf en daube *beef casserole*
bœuf miroton *beef and onion stew*
bœuf mode *beef stew with carrots*
bolet *boletus (mushroom)*
boudin blanc *white pudding*
boudin noir *black pudding*
bouillabaisse *fish soup*
bouilli *boiled*
bouillon *broth*
bouillon de légumes *vegetable stock*
bouillon de poule *chicken stock*
boulette *meatball*
bourride *fish soup*
brandade de morue *cod in cream and garlic*
brioche *round roll*
brochet *pike*
brochette *kebab*
brugnon *nectarine*
brûlot *flambéed brandy*
brut *very dry*

C

cabillaud *cod*
café *coffee (black)*
café complet *continental breakfast*
café crème *coffee with milk*
café glacé *iced coffee*
café liégeois *iced coffee with cream*
caille *quail*
calamar/calmar *squid*
calvados *apple brandy*
canapé *small open sandwich, canapé*

canard *duck*
canard laqué *Peking duck*
caneton *duckling*
cantal *white cheese from Auvergne*
câpres *capers*
carbonnade *beef cooked in beer*
cari *curry*
carotte *carrot*
carottes Vichy *carrots in butter and parsley*
carpe *carp*
carré d'agneau *rack of lamb*
carrelet *flounder*
carte *menu*
carte des vins *wine list*
casse-croûte *snacks*
cassis *black currant*
cassoulet *bean, pork, and duck casserole*
céleri *celery*
céleri rave *celeriac*
céleri en branches *celery*
cèpe *cep (mushroom)*
cerise *cherry*
cerises à l'eau de vie *cherries in brandy*
cervelle *brains*
chabichou *goat's and cow's milk cheese*
chablis *dry white wine from Burgundy*
champignon *mushroom*
champignon de Paris *white button mushroom*
chanterelle *chanterelle (mushroom)*
chantilly *whipped cream*
charcuterie *sausages, ham, and pâtés; pork products*
charlotte *dessert with fruit, cream, and cookies*
chausson aux pommes *apple turnover*
cheval *horse*
chèvre *goat's cheese*
chevreuil *venison*
chicorée *endive*
chocolat chaud *hot chocolate*
chocolat glacé *chocolate ice cream*

chou cabbage
chou à la crème cream puff
choucroute sauerkraut with sausages and ham
chou-fleur cauliflower
chou rouge red cabbage
choux de Bruxelles Brussels sprouts
cidre cider
cidre doux sweet cider
citron lemon
citron pressé fresh lemon juice
civet de lièvre hare stew
clafoutis baked batter pudding with fruit
cochon de lait suckling pig
cocktail de crevettes prawn cocktail
cœur heart
coing quince
colin hake
compote stewed fruit
comté hard cheese from the Jura
concombre cucumber
confit de canard duck preserved in fat
confit d'oie goose preserved in fat
confiture jam
congre conger eel
consommé clear meat or chicken soup
coq au vin chicken in red wine
coque cockle
coquelet cockerel
coquilles Saint-Jacques scallops in cream sauce
côte de porc pork chop
côtelette chop
cotriade bretonne fish soup from Brittany
coulommiers rich, soft cheese
court-bouillon fish stock
crabe crab
crème cream; creamy sauce or dessert; white (coffee)
crème à la vanille vanilla custard
crème anglaise custard
crème chantilly whipped cream
crème d'asperges cream of asparagus soup
crème de bolets cream of mushroom soup
crème de volaille cream of chicken soup
crème d'huîtres cream of oyster soup
crème fouettée whipped cream
crème pâtissière rich, creamy custard

crème renversée set custard
crème vichyssoise cold leek and potato soup
crêpe pancake
crêpe à la crème de marron pancake with chestnut cream
crêpe à l'œuf pancake with fried egg
crêpe de froment wheat pancake
crêpes Suzette pancakes flambéed with orange sauce
crépinette small sausage patty wrapped in fat
cresson cress
crevette grise shrimp
crevettes bouquet pink shrimp
croque-madame grilled cheese and ham sandwich with a fried egg
croque-monsieur grilled cheese and ham sandwich
crottin de Chavignol small goat's cheese
crustacés shellfish
cuisses de grenouille frogs' legs

D

dartois pastry with jam
dégustation de vin wine tasting
digestif liqueur
dinde turkey
doux sweet

E

eau minérale gazeuse sparkling mineral water
eau minérale plate still mineral water
échalote shallot
écrevisse freshwater crayfish
endive chicory
en papillote baked in foil or paper
entrecôte rib steak
entrecôte au poivre peppered rib steak
entrecôte maître d'hôtel steak with butter and parsley
entrée starter
entremets dessert
épaule d'agneau farcie stuffed shoulder of lamb
épinards en branches leaf spinach
escalope de veau milanaise veal escalope with tomato sauce
escalope panée breaded escalope

escargot snail
estouffade de bœuf beef casserole
estragon tarragon

F

faisan pheasant
farci stuffed
fenouil fennel
filet fillet
filet de bœuf Rossini fillet of beef with foie gras
filet de perche perch fillet
fine fine brandy
flageolets kidney beans
flan custard tart
foie de veau veal liver
foie gras goose or duck liver preserve
foies de volaille chicken livers
fonds d'artichaut artichoke hearts
fondue bourguignonne meat fondue
fondue savoyarde cheese fondue
fraise strawberry
fraise des bois wild strawberry
framboise raspberry
frisée curly lettuce
frit deep-fried
frites chips
fromage cheese
fromage blanc cream cheese
fromage de chèvre goat's cheese
fruits de mer seafood

G

galette round, flat cake or savoury buckwheat crêpe
garni with potatoes and vegetables
gâteau cake
gaufre wafer; waffle
gelée jelly
Gewürztraminer dry white wine from Alsace
gibier game
gigot d'agneau leg of lamb
girolle chanterelle (mushroom)
glace ice cream
goujon gudgeon (fish)
gratin dish baked with milk, cheese, and cream
gratin dauphinois sliced potatoes baked in milk and cream
gratinée baked onion soup
grillé grilled
grondin gurnard (fish)
groseille rouge red currant

H

hachis parmentier *shepherd's pie*
hareng mariné *marinated herring*
haricots *beans*
haricots blancs *haricot beans*
haricots verts *green beans*
homard *lobster*
hors-d'œuvre *starter*
huître *oyster*

I, J, K

îles flottantes *floating islands (soft meringue on custard)*
infusion *herb tea*
jambon *ham*
jambon de Bayonne *smoked and cured ham*
julienne *soup with chopped vegetables*
jus de fruits *fruit juice*
jus de pomme *apple juice*
jus d'orange *orange juice*
kir *white wine with black currant liqueur*
kirsch *cherry brandy*

L

lait *milk*
laitue *lettuce*
langouste *saltwater crayfish*
langoustine *Dublin Bay prawn*
lapereau *young rabbit*
lapin *rabbit*
lapin de garenne *wild rabbit*
lard *bacon*
légume *vegetable*
lentilles *lentils*
lièvre *hare*
limande *lemon sole*
livarot *strong, soft cheese from the north of France*
longe *loin*
lotte *monkfish*
loup au fenouil *bass with fennel*

M

macédoine de légumes *mixed vegetables*
mâche *lamb's lettuce*
mangue *mango*
maquereau *mackerel*
marc *grape brandy*
marcassin *young boar*
marchand de vin *in red wine sauce*
marron *chestnut*
massepain *marzipan*
menthe *peppermint*
menthe à l'eau *mint cordial with water*

menu du jour *today's menu*
menu gastronomique *gourmet menu*
menu touristique *tourist menu*
merlan *whiting*
millefeuille *custard slice*
millésime *vintage*
morille *morel (mushroom)*
morue *cod*
moules *mussels*
moules marinières *mussels in white wine*
mousseux *sparkling*
moutarde *mustard*
mouton *mutton*
mulet *mullet*
munster *strong cheese*
mûre *blackberry*
Muscadet *dry white wine*
myrtille *blueberry*

N

nature *plain*
navarin *mutton stew with vegetables*
navet *turnip*
noisette *hazelnut*
noisette d'agneau *medallion of lamb*
noix *nuts, walnuts*
nouilles *noodles*

O

œuf à la coque *boiled egg*
œuf dur *hard-boiled egg*
œuf mollet *soft-boiled egg*
œuf poché *poached egg*
œufs brouillés *scrambled eggs*
œuf sur le plat *fried egg*
oie *goose*
oignon *onion*
omelette au naturel *plain omelet*
omelette aux fines herbes *herb omelet*
omelette paysanne *omelet with potatoes and bacon*
orange pressée *fresh orange juice*
oseille *sorrel*
oursin *sea urchin*

P

pain *bread*
pain au chocolat *chocolate croissant*
palette de porc *shoulder of pork*
palourde *clam*
pamplemousse *grapefruit*
pastis *anise-flavored alcoholic drink*
pâté de canard *duck pâté*

pâté de foie de volaille *chicken liver pâté*
pâte feuilletée *puff pastry*
pâtes *pasta*
pêche *peach*
perdreau *young partridge*
perdrix *partridge*
petite friture *whitebait*
petit pain *roll*
petit pois *peas*
petits fours *small pastries*
petit suisse *cream cheese*
pied de porc *pig's feet*
pigeonneau *young pigeon*
pignatelle *cheese fritter*
pilaf de mouton *rice dish with mutton*
pintade *guinea fowl*
piperade *dish of egg, tomatoes, and peppers*
pissaladière *Provençal dish similar to pizza*
pistache *pistachio*
plat du jour *dish of the day*
plateau de fromages *cheese board*
pochouse *fish casserole with white wine*
poire *pear*
poireau *leek*
poisson *fish*
poivre *pepper*
poivron *red/green pepper*
pomme *apple*
pomme de terre *potato*
pommes de terre à l'anglaise *boiled potatoes*
pommes de terre en robe de chambre/des champs *baked potatoes*
pommes de terre sautées *fried potatoes*
pommes frites *chips*
pommes paille *finely cut chips*
pommes vapeur *steamed potatoes*
porc *pork*
potage *soup*
potage bilibi *fish and oyster soup*
potage Crécy *carrot and rice soup*
potage au cresson *watercress soup*
potage Ésaü *lentil soup*
potage parmentier *leek and potato soup*
potage printanier *vegetable soup*
potage Saint-Germain *split pea soup*
potage velouté *creamy soup*
pot-au-feu *beef and vegetable stew*
potée *vegetable and meat stew*
Pouilly-Fuissé *dry white wine from Burgundy*

poule au pot *chicken and vegetable stew*
poulet basquaise *chicken with ratatouille*
poulet chasseur *chicken with mushrooms and white wine*
poulet créole *chicken in white sauce with rice*
poulet rôti *roast chicken*
praire *clam*
prune *plum*
pruneau *prune*
pudding *plum pudding*
purée *mashed potatoes*

Q

quenelle *meat or fish dumpling*
queue de bœuf *oxtail*
quiche lorraine *egg, bacon, and cream tart*

R

raclette *Swiss dish of melted cheese*
radis *radish*
ragoût *stew*
raie *skate*
raie au beurre noir *skate fried in butter*
raifort *horseradish*
raisin *grape*
râpé *grated*
rascasse *scorpion fish*
ratatouille *stew of peppers, courgettes, aubergines, and tomatoes*
ravigote *herb dressing*
reblochon *strong cheese from Savoy*
rémoulade *mayonnaise dressing with herbs, mustard, and capers*
rigotte *small goat's cheese from Lyon*
rillettes *potted pork or goose meat*
ris de veau *veal sweetbread*
riz *rice*
riz pilaf *spicy rice with meat or seafood*
rognon *kidney*
roquefort *blue cheese*
rôti *roasted/joint of meat*
rouget *mullet*

S

sabayon *zabaglione (whipped egg yolk in Marsala wine)*
sablé *shortbread*
saignant *rare*
saint-honoré *cream puff cake*
saint-marcellin *creamy cow's cheese*
salade composée *mixed salad*

salade russe *diced vegetables in mayonnaise*
salade verte *green salad*
salmis *game stew*
salsifis *oyster plant, salsify*
sanglier *wild boar*
sauce aurore *white sauce with tomato purée*
sauce béarnaise *thick sauce of eggs and butter with tarragon*
sauce blanche *white sauce*
sauce gribiche *dressing with hard-boiled eggs*
sauce hollandaise *rich sauce of eggs, butter, and vinegar, served with fish*
sauce Madère *Madeira sauce*
sauce matelote *wine sauce*
sauce Mornay *béchamel sauce with cheese*
sauce mousseline *hollandaise sauce with cream*
sauce poulette *sauce of mushrooms and egg yolks*
sauce ravigote *dressing with shallots and herbs*
sauce suprême *creamy sauce*
sauce tartare *mayonnaise with herbs and gherkins*
sauce veloutée *white sauce with egg yolks and cream*
sauce vinot *wine sauce*
saucisse *sausage*
saucisse de Francfort *frankfurter*
saucisse de Strasbourg *beef sausage*
saucisson *salami*
saumon *salmon*
saumon fumé *smoked salmon*
sauternes *sweet white wine*
savarin *rum baba*
sec *dry*
seiche *cuttlefish*
sel *salt*
service (non) compris *service (not) included*
service 12% inclus *12% service charge included*
sole bonne femme *sole in white wine and mushrooms*
sole meunière *floured sole fried in butter*
soupe *soup*
soupe au pistou *thick vegetable soup with basil*
steak au poivre *peppered steak*
steak frites *steak and chips*
steak haché *minced meat, minced beef*
steak tartare *raw minced beef with a raw egg*
sucre *sugar*
suprême de volaille *chicken in cream sauce*

T

tanche *tench (fish)*
tarte aux fraises *strawberry tart*
tarte aux pommes *apple tart*
tarte frangipane *almond cream tart*
tartelette *small tart*
tarte Tatin *baked apple dish*
tartine *bread and butter*
tendrons de veau *breast of veal*
terrine *pâté*
tête de veau *calf's head*
thé *tea*
thé à la menthe *mint tea*
thé au lait *tea with milk*
thé citron *lemon tea*
thon *tuna*
tomates farcies *stuffed tomatoes*
tome de Savoie *white cheese from Savoy*
tournedos *round beef steak*
tourte *covered pie*
tourteau *type of crab*
tripes à la mode de Caen *tripe in spicy vegetable sauce*
truite au bleu *poached trout*
truite aux amandes *trout with almonds*
truite meunière *trout in flour and fried in butte*

V, Y

vacherin *strong, soft cheese from the Jura*
vacherin glacé *ice cream meringue*
veau *veal*
velouté de tomate *cream of tomato soup*
vermicelle *vermicelli (very fine pasta)*
viande *meat*
vin *wine*
vinaigrette *French dressing*
vin blanc *white wine*
vin de pays *local wine*
vin de table *table wine*
vin rosé *rosé wine*
vin rouge *red wine*
volaille *poultry*
VSOP *mature brandy*
yaourt *yogurt*

Dictionary
ENGLISH TO FRENCH

The gender of a singular French noun is indicated by the word for *the*: **le** and **la** (masculine and feminine). If these are abbreviated to **l'** in front of a vowel or the letter *h*, or if the noun is plural, indicated by **les**, then the gender is indicated by the abbreviations (m) or (f). French adjectives (adj) vary according to the gender and number of the word they describe; the masculine form is shown here. In most cases, you add an **-e** to the masculine form to make it feminine. Certain endings use a different rule: masculine adjectives that end in **-x** adopt an **-se** ending in the feminine form, while those that end in **-ien** change to **-ienne**. Some feminine adjectives that do not follow these rules are shown here and follow the abbreviation (fem). For the plural form, a (silent) **-s** is usually added.

A

a **un/une**
about: about sixteen **environ seize**
accelerator **l'accélérateur** (m)
accident **l'accident** (m)
accommodation **l'hébergement** (m)
accountant **le/la comptable**
ache **la douleur**
adaptor (plug) **la prise multiple;** (voltage) **l'adaptateur** (m)
address **l'adresse** (f)
adhesive **l'adhésif** (m)
admission charge **le prix d'entrée**
advance **l'avance** (f)
after **après**
afternoon **l'après-midi** (m/f)
aftershave **l'après-rasage** (m)
again **de nouveau**
against **contre**
agenda **l'ordre du jour** (m)
agent **l'agent** (m)
AIDS **le SIDA**
air **l'air** (m)
air conditioning **la climatisation**
aircraft **l'avion** (m)
airline **la compagnie aérienne**
airmail **par avion**
air mattress **le matelas pneumatique**
airport **l'aéroport** (m)
airport bus **la navette (pour l'aéroport)**
aisle (supermarket) **le rayon**
alarm clock **le réveil**
alcohol **l'alcool** (m)
Algeria **l'Algérie** (f)
Algerian **algérien(ne)**

all **tout**; *all the streets* **toutes les rues**; *that's all* **c'est tout**
allergic **allergique**
almost **presque**
alone (adj) **seul(e)**
Alps **les Alpes** (f)
already **déjà**
always **toujours**
am: I am **je suis**
ambulance **l'ambulance** (f)
America **l'Amérique** (f)
American **américain(e)**
and **et**
Andorra **Andorre** (f)
ankle **la cheville**
another (different) **un/une autre;** *another coffee, please* **encore un café, s'il vous plaît**
answering machine **le répondeur**
antifreeze **l'antigel** (m)
antiques shop **le magasin d'antiquités; l'antiquaire** (m)
antiseptic **l'antiseptique** (m)
apartment **l'appartement** (m)
aperitif **l'apéritif** (m)
appetite **l'appétit** (m)
apple **la pomme**
application form **le formulaire de demande**
appointment **le rendez-vous**
apricot **l'abricot** (m)
April **avril**
architecture **l'architecture** (f)
are: you are (singular informal) **tu es**; *we are* **nous sommes**; (plural; singular formal) **vous êtes**; *they are* **ils/elles sont**
arm **le bras**
armchair **le fauteuil**
arrival **l'arrivée** (f)

arrive (verb) **arriver**
art **l'art** (m)
art gallery **le musée d'art; la galerie d'art**
artist **l'artiste** (m/f)
as: as soon as possible **dès que possible**
ashtray **le cendrier**
asleep **endormi(e)**; *he's asleep* **il dort**
aspirin **l'aspirine** (f)
asthmatic **asthmatique**
at: at the post office **à la poste;** *at the café* **au café;** *at 3 o'clock* **à 3 heures**
ATM **le distributeur automatique**
attic **le grenier**
attractive (adj) **attirant(e)**
audio guide **l'audioguide** (m)
August **août**
aunt **la tante**
Australia **l'Australie** (f)
Australian **australien(ne)**
automatic **automatique**
autumn **l'automne** (m)
avocado **l'avocat** (m)
away: is it far away? **est-ce que c'est loin?;** *go away!* **allez-vous en!**
awful (adj) **affreux(euse)**
ax **la hache**
axle **l'essieu** (m)

B

baby **le bébé**
baby wipes **les lingettes** (f)
back (not front) **l'arrière** (m); (body) **le dos;** *I'll come back tomorrow* **je reviendrai demain**
backpack **le sac à dos**

bacon **le bacon;** *bacon and eggs* **des œufs au bacon**
bad (adj) **mauvais(e)**
baggage **les bagages** (m)
baggage check-in **l'enregistrement des bagages** (m)
baggage claim **la réclamation de bagages**
bait **l'appât** (m)
bake (verb) **cuire**
bakery **la boulangerie**
balcony **le balcon**
bald (adj) **chauve**
ball (football, etc.) **le ballon;** (tennis, etc.) **la balle**
ballpoint pen **le stylo-bille**
banana **la banane**
band (musicians) **le groupe**
bandage **le pansement, le bandage**
bank **la banque**
bar **le bar**
barbecue **le barbecue**
barber's **le coiffeur**
bargain **l'affaire** (f)
basement **le sous-sol**
basin (sink) **le lavabo**
basket **le panier**
bath **le bain;** (bathtub) **la baignoire;** *to have a bath* **prendre un bain**
bathroom **la salle de bains**
battery (car) **la batterie;** (flashlight) **la pile**
be (verb) **être**
beach **la plage**
beans **les haricots** (m)
beard **la barbe**
beautiful (adj) **beau,** (fem) **belle**
because **parce que**
bed **le lit**
bed linen **les draps** (m)
bedroom **la chambre**
beef **le bœuf**
beer **la bière**
before **avant**
beginner **le/la débutant(e)**
beginners' slope **la piste pour débutants**
behind **derrière**
beige **beige**
Belgian **belge**
Belgium **la Belgique**
bell (church) **la cloche;** (door) **la sonnette**
below **sous**
belt **la ceinture**
beside **à côté de**
best: the best **le/la meilleur(e)**
better **mieux**
between **entre**
bicycle **la bicyclette, le vélo**

big (adj) **grand**
bill **l'addition** (f)
bill (paper money) **le billet**
bird **l'oiseau** (m)
birthday **l'anniversaire** (m); *happy birthday!* **joyeux anniversaire!**
bite (by dog) **la morsure;** (by snake) **la piqûre,** (verb: by dog) **mordre;** (verb: by insect, snake) **piquer**
bitter (adj) **amer,** (fem) **amère**
black **noir(e)**
blackberry **la mûre**
black currant **le cassis**
blanket **la couverture**
bleach **l'eau de Javel** (f); (verb) **décolorer**
blind (adj) (cannot see) **aveugle;** (window) **le store**
blister **l'ampoule** (f)
blizzard **la tempête de neige**
blond (adj) **blond**
blood **le sang**
blood test **l'analyse de sang** (f)
blouse **le chemisier**
blue **bleu(e)**
boarding pass **la carte d'embarquement**
boat **le bateau;** (smaller) **la barque**
body **le corps**
boil (verb) **bouillir**
boiled (adj) **bouilli(e)**
boiler **le chauffe-eau**
bolt (on door) **le verrou;** (verb) **verrouiller**
bone **l'os** (m); (fish) **l'arête** (f)
bonnet (car) **le capot**
book **le livre;** (verb) **réserver**
bookshop **la librairie**
boot (footwear) **la botte;** (car) **le coffre**
border **la frontière**
boring (adj) **ennuyeux(euse)**
born: I was born in... **je suis né(e) en...**
both **les deux;** *both of them* **tous les deux;** *both of us* **nous deux;** *both large and small* **grand et petit à la fois**
bottle **la bouteille**
bottle opener **le décapsuleur, l'ouvre bouteille** (m)
bottom **le fond;** (part of body) **le derrière**
bowl **le bol;** (animal) **la gamelle**
box **la boîte**

box office (theater, etc.) **le guichet, la billetterie**
boy **le garçon**
boyfriend **le petit ami**
bra **le soutien-gorge**
bracelet **le bracelet**
braces (clothes) **les bretelles** (f)
brake **le frein;** (verb) **freiner**
branch **la branche**
brandy **le cognac**
bread **le pain**
breakdown (car) **la panne;** (nervous) **la dépression;** *I've had a breakdown* (car) **je suis tombé(e) en panne**
breakfast **le petit déjeuner**
breathe (verb) **respirer**
bricklayer **le/la maçon(ne)**
bridge **le pont**
briefcase **l'attaché-case** (m)
British **britannique**
Brittany **la Bretagne**
brochure **la brochure**
broken (adj) **cassé(e);** *broken leg* **la jambe cassée;** *broken down* **en panne**
brooch **la broche**
brother **le frère**
brown (adj) **marron**
bruise **le bleu**
brush **la brosse;** (paintbrush) **le pinceau;** (broom) **le balai;** (verb) **brosser**
Brussels **Bruxelles**
bucket **le seau**
budget **le budget**
builder **le/la constructeur (trice)**
building **le bâtiment**
bumper **le pare-chocs**
bunker **le bunker**
bureau de change **le bureau de change**
burglary **le cambriolage**
burn **la brûlure;** (verb) **brûler**
bus **le bus**
business **les affaires** (f); *it's none of your business* **cela ne vous regarde pas**
business card **la carte de visite**
bus station **la gare routière**
bus stop **l'arrêt de bus** (m)
busy (adj) (occupied) **occupé(e);** (street) **animé(e)**

but **mais**
butcher's **la boucherie**
butter **le beurre**
button **le bouton**
buy (verb) **acheter**
by: by the window **près
de la fenêtre;** by Friday
d'ici vendredi; by myself
tout seul; written by
écrit par

C

cabbage **le chou**
cabinet **le placard**
cable car **le téléphérique**
cable TV **la télévision
par câble**
café **le café**
cage **la cage**
cake **le gâteau**
cake shop **la pâtisserie**
calculator **la calculette**
call: what's it called?
**comment est-ce que
ça s'appelle?**
camcorder **le caméscope**
camera **l'appareil-photo** (m)
camper van **le camping-car**
campfire **le feu de camp**
campsite **le terrain de
camping**
camshaft **l'arbre à cames** (m)
can (vessel) **la boîte
de conserve;** (to be able)
pouvoir; can I have…? **Je
peux avoir…?;** can you…?
Vous pouvez…?
Canada **le Canada**
Canadian **canadien(ne)**
canal **le canal**
candle **la bougie**
canoe **le canoë**
can opener **l'ouvre-boîte** (m)
cap (hat) **la casquette;**
(bottle) **la capsule**
car **la voiture;** (train)
la voiture, le wagon
caravan **la caravane**
carburettor **le carburateur**
card **la carte**
cardigan **le gilet**
careful (adj) **prudent;** careful!
attention!; be careful!
soyez prudent!
caretaker **le/la concierge**
carpenter **le/la
charpentier(ière)**
carpet **le tapis**
carriage (train) **la voiture**
carrot **la carotte**
car seat (for a baby) **le siège
pour bébé**
case **la valise**

cash **l'argent** (m), les
espèces (f), **le liquide;**
to pay cash **payer
en liquide**
cashier **le guichet**
cassette **la cassette**
cassette player **le lecteur
de cassettes**
castle **le château**
cat **le chat**
cathedral **la cathédrale**
cauliflower **le chou-fleur**
cave **la grotte**
CD **le disque
compact**
ceiling **le plafond**
cellar **la cave**
cell phone **le téléphone
portable**
cemetery **le cimetière**
central heating **le chauffage
central**
center **le centre**
certificate **le certificat**
chair **la chaise**
change (money) **la monnaie;**
(verb: money) **changer;**
(verb: clothes) **se changer**
Channel **la Manche**
Channel Islands **les îles
Anglo-Normandes**
Channel Tunnel **le tunnel
sous la Manche**
charger (cell phone)
le chargeur; (electric car)
la prise
charging cable **le câble
de recharge**
charging point/station **la
borne de recharge**
cheap (adj) **bon marché,
pas cher**
check **le chèque**
checkbook **le carnet
de chèques**
check in (luggage) **faire
enregistrer ses bagages**
check-in **l'enregistrement** (m)
checkout (supermarket)
la caisse
cheers! (toast) **santé!**
cheese **le fromage**
cheese shop **la fromagerie**
cherry **la cerise**
chess **les échecs** (m)
chest **la poitrine**
chest of drawers **la commode**
chicken **le poulet**
child **l'enfant** (m)
children **les enfants** (m)
children's ward **le service
de pédiatrie**
chimney **la cheminée**
china **la porcelaine**

chips **les chips** (f)
chocolate **le chocolat;** a box
of chocolates **la boîte de
chocolats;** chocolate bar
la tablette de chocolat
chop (food) **la côtelette;**
(verb: cut) **couper**
church **l'église** (f)
cigar **le cigare**
cigarette **la cigarette**
city **la ville**
city center **le centre ville**
class **la classe**
classical music **la musique
classique**
clean (adj) **propre**
cleaning staff **l'employé(e)
de ménage**
clear (adj) **clair(e)**
clever (adj) **intelligent(e)**
clock **l'horloge** (f); desk clock
l'horloge de bureau (f);
wall clock **l'horloge
murale** (f)
close **près** (near);
étouffant(e) (stuffy);
(verb) **fermer**
closed (adj) **fermé(e)**
clothes **les vêtements** (m)
clubs (cards) **le trèfle**
clutch **l'embrayage** (m)
coat **le manteau**
coat hanger **le cintre**
cockroach **le cafard**
cocktail party **le cocktail**
coffee **le café;** coffee with
milk **le café crème**
coin **la pièce**
cold (illness) **le rhume;**
(adj) **froid(e)**
collar **le col, le collier**
collection (stamps, etc.)
la collection;
(postal) **la levée**
color **la couleur**
color film **la pellicule
couleur**
comb **le peigne;** (verb)
peigner
come (verb) **venir;** I come
from… **je viens de…;**
we came last week
**nous sommes arrivés
la semaine dernière**
company **la compagnie,
la enterprise**
compartment **le
compartiment**
complicated (adj)
compliqué(e)
computer **l'ordinateur** (m)
concert **le concert**
conditioner (hair) **l'après
shampooing** (m)

condom **le préservatif**
conductor (orchestra) **le/la chef(fe) d'orchestre**
confectioner **le/la confiseur(euse)**
conference **la conférence**
conference room **la salle de conférences**
congratulations! **félicitations!**
consulate **le consulat**
consultant **le/la consultant(e)**
contact lenses **lentilles de contact** (f)
contact solution (for contact lenses) **la solution de trempage**
contraceptive **le contraceptif**
cook **le/la cuisinier(ière)**; (verb) **faire la cuisine**
cooker **la cuisinière**
cookie **le biscuit**
cooking utensils **les utensiles de cuisine** (f)
cool (adj) **frais, (fem) fraîche**
cork **le bouchon**
corkscrew **le tire-bouchon**
corner **le coin**
corridor **le couloir**
Corsica **la Corse**
Corsican **corse**
cosmetics **les produits de beauté** (m)
cost (verb) **coûter;** *how much does it cost?* **combien ça coûte?**
cot **le lit d'enfant**
cotton **le coton**
cotton balls **le coton hydrophile**
cough **la toux;** (verb) **tousser**
country (state) **le pays;** (not town) **la campagne**
cousin **le/la cousin(e)**
cover (blanket) **la couverture**
crab **le crabe**
cramp **la crampe**
crayfish (freshwater) **l'écrevisse** (f); (saltwater) **la langouste**
cream **la crème**
credit card **la carte**
cross over (verb) **traverser**
crowded (adj) **bondé(e)**
cruise **la croisière**
crutches **les béquilles** (f)
cry (verb) (weep) **pleurer;** (shout) **crier**
cucumber **le concombre**
cuff links **les boutons de manchette** (m)
cup **la tasse**
curlers **les rouleaux** (m)
curls **les boucles** (f)

current **le courant**
curry **le curry**
curtain **le rideau**
customs **la douane**
cut **la coupure;** (verb) **couper**
cycling **le vélo**

D

dad **papa**
dairy products **les produits laitiers** (m)
dance **la danse;** (verb) **danser**
dangerous (adj) **dangereux(euse)**
dark **foncé(e);** *dark blue* **bleu foncé**
daughter **la fille**
day **le jour**
dead (adj) **mort(e)**
deaf (adj) **sourd(e)**
dear (adj) **cher, (fem) chère**
debit card **la carte bancaire**
December **décembre**
decorator **le/la décorateur(trice)**
deep (adj) **profond(e)**
delay **le retard**
deliberately **exprès**
delicatessen **la charcuterie**
delivery **la livraison**
dentist **le/la dentiste**
dentures **le dentier**
deny (verb) **nier**
deodorant **le déodorant**
department **la département**
department store **le grand magasin**
departures (airport, etc.) **les départs** (m)
deposit **la caution**
designer **le/la designer**
desk **le bureau**
desserts **les desserts** (m)
develop (verb) **développer**
diabetic **diabétique**
diamond (jewel) **le diamant**
diamonds (cards) **le carreau**
diaper **la couche**
diarrhea **la diarrhée**
diary **l'agenda** (m)
dictionary **le dictionnaire**
die (verb) **mourir**
diesel **le diesel;** le gazole
different **différent(e);** *that's different* **c'est différent;** *I'd like a different one* **j'en voudrais un autre**
difficult **difficile**
dining room **la salle à manger**

dinner **le dîner**
dinner party **le dîner**
directory (telephone) **l'annuaire** (m); **les renseignements** (m)
disabled (adj) **handicapé(e)**
disco **la discothèque**
discount **la réduction**
dishcloth **le torchon**
dish soap **le produit pour la vaisselle**
dishwasher **le lave-vaisselle**
disposable diapers **les couches à jeter** (f)
distributor (car) **le delco**
dive (verb) **plonger**
diving board **le plongeoir**
divorced (adj) **divorcé(e)**
do (verb) **faire;** *how do you do?* **comment allez-vous?**
dock **le quai**
doctor **le docteur;** le/la **médecin**
document **le document**
dog **le chien**
doll **la poupée**
dollar **le dollar**
door (building) **la porte;** (car) **la portière**
double room **la chambre pour deux personnes**
doughnut **le beignet**
down **en bas**
drawer **le tiroir**
dress **la robe**
drink **la boisson;** (verb) **boire;** *would you like a drink?* **vous voulez boire quelque chose?**
drinking water **l'eau potable** (f)
drive (verb: car) **conduire**
driver **le/la conducteur(trice)**
driver's license **le permis de conduire**
driveway **l'allée** (f)
drops **les goutes** (f)
drugstore **la pharmacie**
drunk (adj) **soûl(e), ivre**
dry (adj) **sec, (fem) sèche**
dry cleaner's **le pressing**
during **pendant**
duster **le chiffon à poussière**
duty-free **hors-taxe**
duvet **la couette**

E

each (every) **chaque;** *two euros each* **deux euros pièce**
ear **l'oreille** (f)
early **tôt**

earphones **les écouteurs** (m)
earrings **les boucles d'oreille** (f)
east **l'est** (m)
easy (adj) **facile**
eat (verb) **manger**
egg **l'œuf** (m)
eight **huit**
eighteen **dix-huit**
eighty **quatre-vingt**
either: *either of them* **n'importe lequel;** *either... or...* **soit... soit...**
elastic **élastique**
elbow **le coude**
electric **électrique**
electrician **l'électricien(ne)**
electricity **l'électricité** (f)
eleven **onze**
else: *something else* **autre chose;** *someone else* **quelqu'un d'autre;** *somewhere else* **ailleurs**
email **l'email** (m), **le message, la messagerie électronique**
email address **l'adresse électronique** (f)
embarrassing (adj) **gênant**
embassy **l'ambassade** (f)
embroidery **la broderie**
emerald **l'émeraude** (f)
emergency **l'urgence** (f)
emergency department **le service des urgences**
emergency exit **la sortie de secours**
empty (adj) **vide**
end **la fin**
engaged (couple) **fiancé(e)**
engine (car) **le moteur;** (train) **la locomotive**
engineer **l'ingénieur(e)**
engineering **l'ingénierie** (f)
England **l'Angleterre** (f)
English **anglais(e)**
enlargement **l'agrandissement** (m)
enough **assez**
entertainment **le divertissement**
entrance **l'entrée** (f)
envelope **l'enveloppe** (f)
epileptic **épileptique**
eraser **la gomme**
escalator **l'escalier roulant** (m)
especially **particulièrement**
estimate **l'estimation** (f)
evening **le soir**
every **chaque**
everyone **tout le monde**
everything **tout**
everywhere **partout**

example **l'exemple** (m); *for example* **par exemple**
excellent (adj) **excellent(e)**
excess baggage **l'excédent de bagages** (m)
exchange (verb) **échanger**
exchange rate **le taux de change**
excursion **l'excursion** (f)
excuse me! **pardon!**
executive (in company) **cadre** (m/f)
exhaust (car) **le pot d'echappement**
exhibition **l'exposition** (f)
exit **la sortie**
expensive (adj) **cher,** (fem) **chère**
extension cord **la rallonge**
exterior **l'extérieur** (m); (adj) **extérieur(e)**
eye **l'œil** (m)
eyebrow **le sourcil**
eyes **les yeux** (m)

F

face **le visage**
face mask **le masque**
faint **vague;** *to faint* (verb) **s'évanouir**
fair **la foire;** (adj: just) **juste;** *it's not fair* **ce n'est pas juste**
fan (ventilator) **le ventilateur;** (enthusiast) **le/la fan**
fan belt **la courroie du ventilateur**
fantastic **fantastique**
far **loin;** *how far is it to... ?* **est-ce que... est loin d'ici?**
fare **le prix du billet**
farm **la ferme**
farmer **le/la fermier(ière)**
fashion **la mode**
fast (adj) **rapide**
fat (adj: person) **gros,** (fem) **grosse;** (on meat, etc.) **le gras**
father **le père**
February **février**
feel (verb) (touch) **toucher;** *I feel hot* **j'ai chaud;** *I feel like...* **j'ai envie de...;** *I don't feel good* **je ne me sens pas bien**
feet **les pieds** (m)
felt-tip pen **le feutre**
ferry (small) **le bac;** (large) **le ferry**
fever **la fièvre**
fiancé **le/la fiancé(e)**

field **le champ;** (academic) **le domaine**
fifteen **quinze**
fifty **cinquante**
fig **la figue**
figures **les chiffres** (m)
filling (in tooth) **le plombage;** (in sandwich, cake) **la garniture**
film **le film**
filter paper **le papier filtre**
finger **le doigt**
fire **le feu;** (blaze) **l'incendie** (m)
fire extinguisher **l'extincteur** (m)
fireplace **la cheminée**
fireworks **le feu d'artifice**
first **premier(ière)**
first aid **les premiers soins** (m)
first class **la première classe**
first floor **le premier étage**
first name **le prénom**
fish **le poisson**
fishing **la pêche;** *to go fishing* **aller à la pêche**
fishing rod **la canne à pêche**
fishmonger's **la poissonnerie**
five **cinq**
fizzy water **l'eau gazeuse** (f)
flag **le drapeau**
flash (camera) **le flash**
flat (adj) (level) **plat**
flat tire **le pneu crevé**
flavor **le goût**
flea **la puce**
flight **le vol**
flight attendant **le steward, l'hôtesse de l'air** (f)
flip-flops **les tongs** (f)
flippers **les palmes** (f)
floor (ground) **le plancher;** (storey) **l'étage** (m)
florist **le/la fleuriste**
flour **la farine**
flower **la fleur**
flowerbed **le parterre de fleurs**
flute **la flûte**
fly (insect) **la mouche;** (verb: plane etc) **voler;** (verb: person) **prendre l'avion**
fog **le brouillard**
folk music **la musique folklorique**
food **la nourriture**
food poisoning **l'intoxication alimentaire** (f)
foot **le pied**

for **pour**; *for me* **pour moi**; *what for?* **pour quoi faire?**; *for a week* **pour une semaine**
foreigner **l'étranger(ère)**
forest **la forêt**
forget (verb) **oublier**
fork **la fourchette**
fortnight **quinze jours**
forty **quarante**
fountain pen **le stylo-plume**
four **quatre**
fourteen **quatorze**
fourth **quatrième**
France **la France**
free (adj) (no cost) **gratuit(e)**; (at liberty) **libre**
freezer **le congélateur**
French **français(e)**
French fries **les frites** (f)
Friday **vendredi**
fridge **le frigo**
fried (adj) **frit**
friend **l'ami(e)**
friendly (adj) **amical(e), gentil(e)**
fringe **la frange**
front: in front **devant**
frost **le gel**
frozen foods **les produits surgelés** (m)
fruit **le fruit**
fruit juice **le jus de fruit**
fry (verb) **frire**
frying pan **la poêle**
full (adj) **complet**; *I'm full!* **j'ai l'estomac bien rempli!**
full board **la pension complète**
funny (adj) **drôle**
furnished (adj) **meublé(e)**
furniture **les meubles** (m)

G

garage **le garage**
garbage **les ordures** (f); **les détritus** (m)
garden **le jardin**
garden center **la jardinerie**
garlic **l'ail** (m)
gas **le gaz**
gasoline **l'essence** (f)
gas-permeable lenses **les lentilles semi-souples** (f)
gas station **la station-service**
gate **le portail, la grille**; (at airport) **la porte d'embarquement**
gay **homosexuel(le)**
gear (car) **la vitesse**
gearstick **le levier de vitesse**
gel **le gel**

German **allemand(e)**
Germany **l'Allemagne** (f)
get (verb) (fetch) **aller chercher**; *have you got...?* **avez vous...?**; *to get the train* **prendre le train**; *get back: we get back tomorrow* **nous rentrons demain**; *to get something back* **récupérer quelque chose**
get in (verb) **entrer**; (arrive) **arriver**
get off (verb) (bus, etc.) **descendre**
get on (verb) (bus, etc.) **monter**
get out (verb) **sortir**
get up (verb) **se lever**
gift **le cadeau**
gin **le gin**
ginger **le gingembre**
girl (child) **la fille**; (young woman) **la jeune fille**
girlfriend **la petite amie**
give (verb) **donner**
glad (adj) **heureux(euse)**
glass **le verre**
glasses (spectacles) **les lunettes** (f)
gloves **les gants** (m)
glue **la colle**
go (verb) **aller**
gold **l'or** (m)
golf **le golf**
golf course **le parcours de golf**
good **bon**, (fem) **bonne**; *good!* **bien!**
goodbye **au revoir**
good evening **bonsoir**
government **le gouvernement**
granddaughter **la petite fille**
grandfather **le grand-père**
grandmother **la grand-mère**
grandparents **les grands-parents** (m)
grandson **le petit-fils**
grapes **les raisins** (m)
grass **l'herbe** (f)
gray **gris(e)**
Great Britain **la Grande-Bretagne**
green **vert(e)**
grill **le gril**
grilled (adj) **grillé(e)**
grocery **l'épicerie** (f)
ground floor **le rez-de-chaussée**
groundsheet **le tapis de sol**
guarantee **la garantie**; (verb) **garantir**
guard (train) **le chef/la cheffe de train**

guest **l'invitée(e)**
guide **le/la guide**
guidebook **le guide**
guitar **la guitare**
gun (rifle) **le fusil**; (pistol) **le pistolet**
gutter **la gouttière**

H

hair **les cheveux** (m); *long/short hair* **les cheveux longs/courts**
haircut **la coupe (de cheveux)**
hairdresser **le coiffeur(euse)**
hair dryer **le sèche-cheveux**
hairspray **la laque**
half **demi**; *half an hour* **une demi-heure**
half board **la demi-pension**
ham **le jambon**
hamburger **le hamburger**
hammer **le marteau**
hamster **le hamster**
hand **la main**
hand luggage **le bagage à main**
hand sanitizer **le désinfectant pour les mains**
handbag **le sac à main**
handbrake **le frein à main**
handkerchief **le mouchoir**
handle (door) **la poignée**
handsome (adj) **beau**
hangover **la gueule de bois**
happy (adj) **heureux(euse)**
harbor **le port**
hard (adj) **dur(e)**; (difficult) **difficile**
hard lenses **les lentilles rigides** (f)
hardware shop **la quincaillerie**
hat **le chapeau**
hate **déteste**
have (verb) **avoir**; *have you got...?* **avez-vous...?**
hay fever **le rhume des foins**
he **il**
head **la tête**
head office **le siège social**
headache **le mal à la tête**
headlights **les phares** (m)
headphones **le casque**
hear (verb) **entendre**
hearing aid **l'appareil auditif** (m)
hearing loop **les boucles magnétiques** (f)
heart **le cœur**
heart condition **le problème cardiaque**

hearts (cards) **cœurs** (m)
heater **le radiateur**
heating **le chauffage**
heavy (adj) **lourd(e)**
hedge **la haie**
heel **le talon**
hello **bonjour**
help **l'aide** (f); (verb) **aider**
hepatitis **l'hépatite** (f)
her: it's for her **c'est pour
elle**; *give it to her* **donnez-
le-lui** *her: her book* **son
livre**; *her house* **sa maison**;
her shoes **ses chaussures**;
it's hers **c'est à elle**
hi **salut**
high (adj) **haut(e)**
hiking **la randonnée**
hill **la colline**
him: it's for him **c'est pour
lui**; *give it to him* **donnez-
le-lui** *his: his book* **son
livre**; *his house* **sa maison**;
his shoes **ses chaussures**;
it's his **c'est à lui**
history **l'histoire** (f)
hitchhike (verb) **faire
de l'autostop**
HIV positive **séropositif(ve)**
hobby **le passe-temps**
holiday **les vacances** (f)
home: at home (my home)
chez moi; *he's at home* **il
est chez lui**
homeopathy **l'homéopathie** (f)
honest (adj) **honnête**
honey **le miel**
honeymoon **la lune de miel**
horn (car) **le klaxon**;
(animal) **la corne**
horrible (adj) **horrible**
hose **le tuyau**
hospital **l'hôpital** (m)
host **l'hôte** (m)
hostess **l'hôtesse** (f)
hot (adj) **chaud(e)**
hotel **l'hôtel** (m)
hour **l'heure** (f)
house **la maison**
household products **les
produits d'entretien** (m)
housekeeping (at a hotel)
le personnel de chambre
hovercraft **l'aéroglisseur** (m)
hoverport **l'hoverport** (m)
how? **comment?**
how much? **combien?**
hundred **cent**
hungry: I'm hungry **j'ai faim**
*hurry: I'm in a hurry
je suis pressé(e)**
husband **le mari**
hydrofoil **l'hydrofoil** (m)

I

I **je**
ice **la glace**
ice cream **la glace**
ice rink **la patinoire**
ice skates **les patins
à glace** (m)
ice-skating: to go ice-skating
aller patiner
identification **la pièce
d'identité**
if **si**
ignition **l'allumage** (m)
ill (adj) **malade**
immediately **immédiatement**
impossible **impossible**
in **dans**; *in France* **en France**
indicator **le clignotant**
indigestion **l'indigestion** (f)
inexpensive (adj) **bon
marché, pas cher**
infection **l'infection** (f)
information **l'information** (f)
injection **la piqûre**
injury **la blessure**
ink **l'encre** (f)
inn **l'auberge** (f)
inner tube **la chambre à air**
insect **l'insecte** (m)
insect repellent **la crème
anti-insecte**
insomnia **l'insomnie** (f)
instant coffee **le café soluble**
insurance **l'assurance** (f)
interesting (adj) **intéressant(e)**
Internet **l'internet** (m)
interpret (verb) **interpréter**
interpreter **l'interprète** (m/f)
invitation **l'invitation** (f)
invoice **la facture**
Ireland **l'Irlande** (f)
Irish **irlandais(e)**
iron (for clothes) **le fer
à repasser**; (verb)
repasser
is: he/she is **il/elle est**;
it is **c'est**
island **l'île** (f)
it **il; elle**
Italian **italien(ne)**
Italy **l'Italie** (f)
its **son; sa; ses** (see his)

J

jacket **la veste**
jam **la confiture**
January **janvier**
jazz **le jazz**
jeans **les jeans** (m)
jellyfish **la méduse**
jeweler's **la bijouterie**
job **le travail**

jog (verb) **faire du jogging**;
to go for a jog **aller faire
du jogging**
joke **la plaisanterie**
journey **le voyage**
July **juillet**
June **juin**
just: it's just arrived **ça vient
juste d'arriver**; *I've got
just one left* **il ne m'en
reste qu'un**

K

kettle **la bouilloire**
key **la clé**
keyboard **le clavier**
kidney **le rein**
kilo **le kilo**
kilometer **le kilomètre**
kind (adj) **gentil(le)**
kitchen **la cuisine**
knee **le genou**
knife **le couteau**
knit (verb) **tricoter**
knitting needle **l'aiguille
à tricoter** (f)
know (verb) (fact) **savoir**;
(person) **connaître**; *I don't
know* **je ne sais pas**

L

label **l'étiquette** (f)
lace **la dentelle**; (of shoe)
le lacet
lake **le lac**
lamb **l'agneau** (m)
lamp **la lampe**
lampshade
l'abat-jour (m)
land **la terre**; (verb)
atterrir
language **la langue**
laptop **l'ordinateur
portable** (m)
large (adj) **grand**
last (final) **dernier(ière)**;
last week **la semaine
dernière**; *at last!* **enfin!**
late tard; the bus is late
le bus est en retard
later **plus tard**
laugh (verb) **rire**
laundromat **la laverie
automatique**
laundry (place) **la
blanchisserie**; (clothes)
le linge
law (subject) **le droit**
lawn **la pelouse**
lawn mower **la tondeuse
à gazon**
lawyer **l'avocat(e)**

laxative **le laxatif**

lazy (adj) **paresseux(euse)**

lead **la laisse**

leaf **la feuille**

leaflet **le dépliant**

learn (verb) **apprendre**

leather **le cuir**

lecture hall **l'amphithéâtre** (m)

leek **le poireau**

left (not right) **la gauche**; there's nothing left **il ne reste plus rien**

leg **la jambe**

lemon **le citron**

lemonade **la limonade**

length **la longueur**

lens (camera) **l'objectif** (m)

less **moins**

lesson **la leçon**

letter **la lettre**

lettuce **la laitue**

library **la bibliothèque**

license **le permis**

license plate **la plaque d'immatriculation**

life **la vie**

lift **l'ascenseur** (m)

light **la lumière**; (adj) (not heavy) **léger**, (fem) **légère**; (adj) (not dark) **clair(e)**

light bulb **l'ampoule** (f)

lighter **le briquet**

lighter fluid **le gaz à briquet**

light meter **la cellule photoélectrique**

like (verb) **aimer**: I like swimming **j'aime nager**; I don't like **je n'aime pas**; (similar to) **comme**

lime (fruit) **le citron vert**

lipstick **le rouge à lèvres**

liqueur **la liqueur**

list **la liste**

liter **le litre**

literature **la littérature**

litter **les ordures** (f)

little (adj) (small) **petit**; it's a little big **c'est un peu trop grand**; just a little **juste un peu**

liver **le foie**

living room **le salon**

lobster **le homard**

lollipop **la sucette**

long (adj) **long**, (fem) **longue**

lost property **les objets trouvés** (m)

loud (adj) **fort(e)**; (color) **criard(e)**

love **l'amour** (m); (verb) **aimer**

lover **l'amant** (m)

low (adj) **bas(se)**

luck **la chance**; good luck! **bonne chance!**

luggage **les bagages** (m)

luggage lockers **la consigne automatique**

luggage rack **le porte-bagages**

lunch **le déjeuner**

Luxembourg **le Luxembourg**

M

mad **fou**, (fem) **folle**

madam **madame**

magazine **la revue**

mailbox **la boîte aux lettres**

main courses **les plats** (m)

make (verb) **faire**

makeup **le maquillage**

man **l'homme** (m)

manager **le/la directeur(trice)**; **le/la chef(fe)**

many **beaucoup**; not many **pas beaucoup**

map **la carte**; (town map) **le plan**; online map **la carte en ligne**

March **mars**

margarine **la margarine**

market **le marché**; indoor market **le marché couvert**

marmalade **la marmelade d'oranges**

married (adj) **marié(e)**

mascara **le mascara**

mask (face) **le masque**

mass (church) **la messe**

mast **le mât**

match (light) **l'allumette** (f); (sport) **le match**

material (cloth) **le tissu**

matter: it doesn't matter **ça ne fait rien**

mattress **le matelas**

May **mai**

maybe **peut-être**

me: it's me **c'est moi**; it's for me **c'est pour moi**; give it to me **donnez-le moi**

meal **le repas**

mean: what does this mean? **qu'est-ce que cela veut dire?**

meat **la viande**

mechanic **le/la mécanicien(ne)**, **le/la garagiste**

medication **les médicaments** (m)

medicine **le médicament**; (subject) **le médicine**

Mediterranean **la Méditerranée**

meeting **la réunion**

melon **le melon**

menu **la carte**; set menu **le menu**

message **le message**

microwave **le micro-ondes**

middle **le milieu**

midnight **le minuit**

milk **le lait**

mine: it's mine **c'est à moi**

mineral water **l'eau minérale** (f)

minute **la minute**

mirror **le miroir**; (car) **le rétroviseur**

Miss **Mademoiselle**

mistake **l'erreur** (f); (verb) to be mistaken **se tromper**

modem **le modem**

Monday **lundi**

money **l'argent** (m)

monitor (computer) **le moniteur**

month **le mois**; months of the year **les mois de l'année**

monument **le monument**

moon **la lune**

moped **la mobylette**

more **plus**; more or less **plus ou moins**

morning **le matin**; in the morning **dans la matinée**

mosquito **le moustique**

mother **la mère**

motorboat **le bateau à moteur**

motorcycle **la moto**

motorway **l'autoroute** (f)

mountain **la montagne**

mountain bike **le vélo tout terrain**

mouse **la souris**

mousse (hair) **la mousse**

moustache **la moustache**

mouth **la bouche**

move (verb) **bouger**; (house) **déménager**; don't move! **ne bougez pas!**

movie theater **le cinéma**

Mr. **Monsieur**

Mrs. **Madame**

mug **la tasse**

museum **le musée**

mushroom **le champignon**

music **la musique**; loud music **la musique forte**

musical instrument **l'instrument de musique** (m)

musician **le/la musicien(ne)**
mussels **les moules** (f)
must: I must **je dois**
mustard **la moutarde**
my: my book **mon livre**;
my house **ma maison**;
my shoes **mes
chaussures**

N

nail (metal) **le clou**;
(finger) **l'ongle** (m)
nail clippers **la pince
à ongles**
nail file **la lime à ongles**
nail polish **le vernis à
ongles**
name **le nom**; what's your
name **comment vous
appelez-vous?**
narrow (adj) **étroit(e)**
near: near the door **près
de la porte**
necessary **nécessaire**
neck **le cou**
necklace **le collier**
need (verb) **avoir besoin
de**; I need… **j'ai besoin
de…**; there's no
need **ce n'est pas
nécessaire**
needle **l'aiguille** (f)
negative (photo) **le
négatif**
neither: neither of them **ni
l'un ni l'autre**; neither…
nor… **ni… ni…**
nephew **le neveu**
never **jamais**
new **nouveau**, (fem)
nouvelle; neuf, (fem)
neuve
news **les nouvelles** (f);
(television) **les
informations** (f)
newspaper **le journal**
newsstand **le tabac**;
le tabac-journaux
next **prochain(e)**; next week
la semaine prochaine;
what next? **et puis quoi?**
nice (adj: place etc) **joli(e)**;
(person) **sympathique**
niece **la nièce**
night **la nuit**
nightclub **la boîte de nuit**
nightdress **la chemise
de nuit**
nine **neuf**
nineteen **dix-neuf**
ninety **quatre-vingt-dix**
no (response) **non**;
(not any) **aucun**

nobody **personne**
noisy (adj) **bruyant(e)**
none **aucun**
noon **le midi**
north **le nord**
nose **le nez**
not **pas**; he's not… **il
n'est pas…**
notebook **le carnet**
notepad **le bloc notes**
nothing **rien**
novel **le roman**
November **novembre**
now **maintenant**
nowhere **nulle part**
nudist **le/la nudiste**
number (figure) **le numéro**;
(amount) **le nombre**
nurse **l'infirmier(ière)**
nut (fruit) **la noix**; (for bolt)
l'écrou (m)

O

oars **les rames** (f)
occasionally **de temps
en temps**
October **octobre**
of **de**
of course **bien sûr**
office **le bureau**
often **souvent**
oil **l'huile** (f)
ointment **la pommade**
OK **d'accord**
old (adj) **vieux**, (fem) **vieille**;
how old are you? **quel
âge avez-vous?**
olive **l'olive** (f)
omelet **l'omelette** (f)
on **sur**
one **un/une**
onion **l'oignon** (m)
only **seulement**
open (adj) **ouvert(e)**;
(verb) **ouvrir**
opening times **les
heures d'ouverture** (f)
operating room **la salle
d'opérations**
operation **l'opération** (f)
operator (phone)
l'opérateur(trice) (m)
opposite **en face de**
optician's **l'opticien(ne)**
or **ou**
orange (fruit) **l'orange** (f);
(color) **orange**
orange juice **le jus
d'orange**
orchestra **l'orchestre** (m)
ordinary **habituel(le)**
organ (music) **l'orgue** (m)
other: the other… **l'autre…**

our: our house **notre
maison**; our children **nos
enfants**; it's ours **c'est
à nous**
out: he's out **il n'est
pas là**
outside **dehors**
oven **le four**
over (above) **au-dessus de**;
(more than) **plus de**;
(finished) **fini(e)**; it's over
the road **c'est de l'autre
côté de la rue**;
over there **là-bas**
overtake (verb) (in a car)
doubler
oyster **l'huître** (f)

P

pack of cards **le jeu de
cartes**
package **le paquet**;
(parcel) **le colis**
packet **le paquet**
padlock **le cadenas**
page **la page**
pain **la douleur**
paint **la peinture**;
(verb) **peindre**
painting **la peinture**
pair **la paire**
pajamas **le pyjama**
palace **le palais**
pale (adj) **pâle, blême**
pancake **la crêpe**
paper **le papier**;
(newspaper) **le journal**
paraffin **le pétrole**
parcel **le colis**
pardon? **pardon?**
parents **les parents** (m)
park **le jardin public**;
(verb) **garer**
parking lot **le parking**
parting (in hair) **la raie**
party (celebration) **la fête,
la soirée**; (group) **le
groupe**; (political) **le parti**
passenger **le/la passager(ère)**
passport **le passeport**
passport control **le contrôle
des passeports**
password **le mot de passe**
pasta **les pâtes** (f)
path **le chemin, l'allée** (f)
pavement **le trottoir**
pay (verb) **payer**
payment **le paiement**;
contactless payment
le paiement sans contact
peach **la pêche**
peanuts **les cacahuètes** (f)
pear **la poire**

pearl **la perle**
peas **les petits pois** (m)
pedestrian **le piéton**
peg **la pince à linge**
pen **le stylo**
pencil **le crayon**
pencil sharpener
   le taille-crayon
penknife **le canif**
pen pal **le/la**
   correspondant(e)
people **les gens** (m)
pepper (and salt) **le poivre;**
   (bell pepper) **le poivron**
peppermints **les**
   bonbons à la
   menthe (m)
per night **par nuit**
perfect (adj) **parfait(e)**
perfume **le parfum**
perhaps **peut-être**
perm **la permanente**
pet passport **le passeport**
   pour animaux
pets **les animaux**
   (familiers) (m)
phone card **la carte**
   téléphonique
photocopier **le copieur**
photograph **la photo;**
   (verb) **photographier**
photographer **le/la**
   photographe
phrase book **le guide**
   de conversation
piano **le piano**
pickpocket **le/la**
   pickpocket
picnic **le pique-nique**
piece **le morceau**
pill **le comprimé**
pillow **l'oreiller** (m)
pilot **le/la pilote**
PIN **le code**
pin **l'épingle** (f)
pineapple **l'ananas** (m)
pink **rose**
pipe (for smoking) **la pipe;**
   (for water) **le tuyau**
piston **le piston**
pitch **l'emplacement** (m)
pizza **la pizza**
place **l'endroit** (m);
   at your place **chez vous**
plant **la plante**
plaster **le pansement**
plastic **le plastique**
plastic bag **le sac**
plastic wrap **le film**
   étirable
plate **l'assiette** (f)
platform **le quai**
play (theater) **la pièce;**
   (verb) **jouer**

please **s'il vous plaît**
pleased: pleased to meet
   you **enchanté(e)**
plug (electrical) **la prise;**
   (sink) **le bouchon**
plumber (occupation)
   le/la plombier(ière)
pocket **la poche**
poison **le poison**
police **la police**
police officer **le/la**
   policier(ière)
police report **le rapport**
   de police
police station **le**
   commissariat
politics **la politique**
poor (adj) **pauvre;**
   (bad quality) **mauvais(e)**
pop music **la musique pop**
pork **le porc**
port (harbor) **le port;**
   (drink) **le porto**
porter **le/la porteur(euse)**
possible **possible**
post **la poste;** (verb) **poster**
postcard **la carte postale**
poster (outside) **l'affiche** (f);
   (inside) **le poster**
postman **le/la facteur(trice)**
post office **la poste**
potato **la pomme de terre**
poultry **la volaille**
pound (money, weight) **la**
   livre
powder **la poudre**
powdered detergent **la**
   lessive
pram **le landau**
prefer (verb) **préférer**
prescription **l'ordonnance** (f)
pretty (adj) (beautiful)
   joli(e); (quite) **plutôt**
price **le prix**
priest **le prêtre**
printer **l'imprimante** (f)
private (adj) **privé(e)**
problem **le problème**
profession **la profession**
professor **le/la professeur(e)**
profits **les bénéfices** (m)
public **le public**
pull (verb) **tirer**
puncture **la crevaison**
purple **violet(te)**
purse **le porte-monnaie**
push (verb) **pousser**
put (verb) **mettre**

Q

quality **la qualité**
quarter **le quart**
question **la question**

queue **la queue;** (verb)
   faire la queue
quick (adj) **rapide**
quiet (adj: person)
   silencieux(euse);
   (street, etc) **tranquille**
quite (fairly) **assez;**
   (fully) **très**
quotation **le devis**

R

rabbit **le lapin**
radiator **le radiateur**
radio **la radio**
radish **le radis**
rail: by rail **par chemin**
   de fer
railway **le chemin**
   de fer
rain **la pluie**
raincoat **l'imperméable** (m)
raisin **le raisin sec**
rake **le râteau**
rare (adj) (uncommon) **rare;**
   (steak) **saignant**
rash **la rougeur**
raspberry **la framboise**
rat **le rat**
razor blades **les lames**
   de rasoir (f)
read (verb) **lire**
reading lamp **la lampe de**
   bureau; (bedside) **la**
   lampe de chevet
ready (adj) **prêt(e)**
ready meals **les plats**
   préparés (m)
receipt **le reçu**
reception **la réception**
receptionist **le/la**
   receptionniste
record (music) **le disque;**
   (sports etc) **le record**
record player **le tourne-**
   disque
record shop **le/la**
   disquaire
red **rouge;** (hair) **roux**
refreshments **les**
   rafraîchissements (m)
registered post **en**
   recommandé
relax (verb) **se détendre**
religion **la religion**
remember (verb) I remember
   je m'en souviens; I don't
   remember **je ne me**
   souviens pas
rent (verb) **louer**
reservation **la réservation**
reserve (verb) **réserver**
rest (remainder) **le reste;**
   (verb: relax) **se reposer**

restaurant **le restaurant**
restaurant car **le wagon-restaurant**
return (verb) (come back) **revenir;** (give back) **rendre**
return ticket **l'aller retour** (m)
rice **le riz**
rich (adj) **riche**
right (adj) (correct) **juste;** (not left) **la droite**
ring (jewelry) **la bague**
ripe (adj) **mûr(e)**
river **la rivière;** (big) **le fleuve**
road **la route;** (in town) **la rue**
roasted (adj) **rôti(e)**
rock (stone) **le rocher;** (music) **le rock**
roll (bread) **le petit pain**
roof **le toit**
room **la chambre;** (space) **la place**
room service **le room service**
rope **la corde**
rose **la rose**
round (adj) (circular) **rond(e);** it's my round **c'est ma tournée;** roundabout **le rond-point**
row (verb) **ramer**
rowing boat **la barque**
rubber (material) **le caoutchouc**
rubber band **l'élastique** (m)
rubber boots **les bottes en caoutchouc** (f)
rug (carpet) **le tapis**
rugby **le rugby**
ruins **les ruines** (f)
ruler **la règle**
rum **le rhum**
run (verb) **courir**
runway **la piste**

S

sad (adj) **triste**
safe (adj) (not in danger) **en sécurité;** (not dangerous) **sans danger**
safety pin **l'épingle à nourrice** (f)
sailing **la voile**
sailing boat **le voilier**
salad **la salade**
sale **la vente;** (at reduced prices) **les soldes** (f)
salmon **le saumon**
salt **le sel**
same: the same... **le/la même...;** the same again, please **la même chose, s'il vous plaît**

sand **le sable**
sandals **les sandales** (f)
sand dunes **les dunes** (f)
sandwich **le sandwich**
sanitary napkins **les serviettes hygiéniques** (f)
Saturday **samedi**
sauce **la sauce**
saucer **la soucoupe**
saucepan **la casserole**
sauna **le sauna**
sausage **la saucisse**
say (verb) **dire;** what did you say? **qu'avez-vous dit?;** how do you say...? **comment dit-on...?**
scarf **l'écharpe** (f); (head) **le foulard**
schedule **l'emploi du temps** (m)
school **l'école** (f)
science **la science**
scissors **les ciseaux** (m)
Scotland **l'Écosse** (f)
screen **l'écran** (m)
screw **la vis**
screwdriver **le tournevis**
sea **la mer**
seafood **les fruits de mer** (m)
seat **la place**
seat belt **la ceinture de sécurité**
second (of time) **la seconde;** (in series) **deuxième**
second class **en seconde**
secretary **le/la secrétaire**
see (verb) **voir;** I can't see **je ne vois rien;** I see **je vois**
self-employed **à mon compte**
sell (verb) **vendre**
seminar **le séminaire**
send (verb) **envoyer**
separate (adj) **séparé(e);** (verb) **séparer**
September **septembre**
serious (adj) **sérieux(euse)**
seven **sept**
seventeen **dix-sept**
seventy **soixante-dix**
several **plusieurs**
sew (verb) **coudre**
shampoo **le shampooing**
shave (verb) to shave **se raser**
shaving cream **la mousse à raser**
shawl **le châle**
she **elle**
sheet **le drap**
shell **la coquille**
shellfish **les crustacés** (m)
ship **le bateau**
shirt **la chemise**
shoelaces **les lacets** (m)

shoemaker **la cordonnerie**
shoe polish **le cirage**
shoes **les chaussures** (f)
shop **le magasin**
shopkeeper **le/la commerçant(e)**
shopping **les courses** (f); to go shopping **faire les courses**
short (adj) **court(e); petit(e)**
shorts **le short**
shoulder **l'épaule** (f)
shower (bath) **la douche;** (rain) **l'averse** (f)
shower gel **le gel douche**
shrimp **la crevette**
shutter (camera) **l'obturateur** (m); (window) **le volet**
sick (adj) I feel sick **j'ai envie de vomir;** to be sick (verb: vomit) **vomir**
side (edge) **le bord**
sidelights **les feux de position** (m)
sightseeing **le tourisme**
silk **la soie**
silver (color) **argenté(e);** (metal) **l'argent** (m)
simple (adj) **simple**
sing (verb) **chanter**
single (one) **seul(e);** (adj) (unmarried) **célibataire**
single room **la chambre pour une personne; la chambre simple**
single ticket **l'aller simple** (m)
sink **l'évier** (m)
sir **monsieur**
sister **la sœur**
six **six**
sixteen **seize**
sixty **soixante**
size **la taille**
skates **les patins à glace** (m)
ski **le ski;** (verb) **skier**
ski boots **les chaussures de ski** (f)
skid (verb) **déraper**
skiing: to go skiing (verb) **faire du ski**
ski lift **le remonte-pente**
skin cleanser **le démaquillant**
ski pole **le bâton de ski**
ski resort **la station de ski**
skirt **la jupe**
sky **le ciel**
sled **la luge**
sleep **le sommeil;** (verb) **dormir**
sleeping bag **le sac de couchage**
sleeping car **le wagon-lit**
sleeping pill **le somnifère**
sleeve **la manche**

slip **le jupon**
slippers **les pantoufles** (f)
slow (adj) **lent(e)**
small (adj) **petit(e)**
smell **l'odeur** (f); (verb) **sentir**
smile **le sourire**; (verb) **sourire**
smoke **la fumée**; (verb) **fumer**
snack **le snack**
sneakers **les tennis** (f)
snow **la neige**
so **alors**
soap **le savon**
soccer **le football**; soccer cleats **les chaussures de football** (f)
socks **les chaussettes** (f)
soft (adj) **mou**, (fem) **molle**
soft lenses **les lentilles souples** (f)
soil **la terre**
somebody **quelqu'un**
somehow **d'une façon ou d'une autre**
something **quelque chose**
sometimes **quelquefois**
somewhere **quelque part**
son **le fils**
song **la chanson**
sorry (apology) **pardon**; sorry? (pardon?) **pardon?**; I'm sorry **je suis désolé(e)**
soup **la soupe**
south **le sud**
souvenir **le souvenir**
spade (shovel) **la pelle**; (garden) **la bêche**
spades (cards) **le pique**
Spain **l'Espagne** (f)
Spanish **espagnol(e)**
spare parts **les pièces de rechange** (f)
spark plug **la bougie**
speak (verb) **parler**; do you speak...? **parlez-vous...?**; I don't speak... **je ne parle pas...**
spectacles (glasses) **les lunettes** (f)
speed **la vitesse**
speed limit **la limitation de vitesse**
spider **l'araignée** (f)
spinach **les épinards** (m)
spoon **la cuillère**
sport **le sport**
sports center **le centre sportif**
spring (mechanical) **le ressort**; (season) **le printemps**
square (in town) **la place**; (adj: shape) **carré(e)**
stadium **le stade**
staircase **l'escalier** (m)

stairs **les escaliers** (m)
stamp **le timbre**
stapler **l'agrafeuse** (f)
star **l'étoile** (f); (movie) **la vedette**
start (beginning) **le début**; (verb) **commencer**
starters **les entrées** (f)
statement **la déposition**
station **la gare**; (underground) **la station**
statue **la statue**
steak **le steak**
steal (verb) **voler**; it's been stolen **on l'a volé(e)**
steamed (adj) **à la vapeur**
steamer **le bateau à vapeur**; (cooking) **le couscoussier**
steering wheel **le volant**
sting **la piqûre**; (verb) **piquer**
stockings **les bas** (m)
stomach **l'estomac** (m)
stomachache **le mal de ventre**, **le mal à l'estomac**
stop (bus) **l'arrêt (de bus)** (m); (verb) **s'arrêter**
storm **la tempête**
straight on **tout droit**
strawberry **la fraise**
stream (small river) **le ruisseau**
street **la rue**
street musician **le/la musicien(ne) des rues**
string (cord) **la ficelle**; (guitar, etc.) **la corde**
stroller **la poussette**
strong (adj: person, drink) **fort(e)**; (material) **résistant(e)**
student **l'étudiant(e)**
stupid (adj) **stupide**
suburbs **la banlieue**
sugar **le sucre**
suit **le costume**; it suits you **ça vous va bien**
suitcase **la valise**
summer **l'été** (m)
sun **le soleil**
sunbathe (verb) **se faire bronzer**
sunburn **le coup de soleil**
Sunday **dimanche**
sunglasses **les lunettes de soleil** (f)
sunny (adj) **ensoleillé(e)**
sunshade **le parasol**
suntan **le bronzage**
suntan lotion **la lotion solaire**
supermarket **le supermarché**

supper **le souper**
supplement **le supplément**
suppository **le suppositoire**
sure **sûr(e)**
surname **le nom de famille**
sweat **la transpiration**; (verb) **transpirer**
sweater **le pull**
sweatshirt **le sweat-shirt**
sweet (adj) (not sour) **sucré(e)**; (confectionery) **bonbon**
swim (verb) **nager**
swimming **la natation**; to go swimming **aller se baigner**
swimming pool **la piscine**
swimming trunks **le maillot de bain**
swimsuit **le maillot de bain**
Swiss (adj) **suisse** (m/f)
switch **l'interrupteur** (m)
Switzerland **la Suisse**
synagogue **la synagogue**
syringe **la seringue**
syrup **le sirop**

T

T-shirt **le tee-shirt**
table **la table**
tablet **le cachet**
take (verb) **prendre**
take away (verb) to take away **à emporter**
takeoff **le décollage**
talcum powder **le talc**
talk **la conversation**; (verb) **parler**
tall (adj) **grand(e)**
tampon **le tampon**
tangerine **la mandarine**
tap (water) **le robinet**
tapestry **la tapisserie**
taxi **le taxi**
tea **le thé**
teacher (secondary) **le/la professeur(e)**
telephone **le téléphone**; (verb) **téléphoner**
telephone box **la cabine téléphonique**
television **la télévision**
temperature **la température**
ten **dix**
tennis **le tennis**
tent **la tente**
tent peg **le piquet de tente**
tent pole **le montant de tente**
terminal **le terminal**
terrace **la terrasse**
than **que**

thank (verb) **remercier;**
thank you **merci;**
thanks **merci**
that (that one) **ça;**
that bus **ce bus;**
that man **cet homme;**
that woman **cette femme;**
what's that? **qu'est-ce que c'est?;** I think that the... **je pense que le...**
the **le/la;** (plural) **les**
theater **le théâtre**
their: their room **leur chambre;** their books **leurs livres;** it's theirs **c'est à eux**
them: it's them **ce sont eux/elles;** it's for them **c'est pour eux/elles;** give it to them **donnez-le-leur**
then **alors;** (after) **ensuite**
there **là;** there is/are... **il y a...**
these: these things **ces choses;** these are mine **ils sont à moi**
they **ils;** (fem) **elles**
thick (adj) **épais(se)**
thief **le/la voleur(euse)**
thin (adj) **maigre, mince**
think (verb) **penser;** I think so **je pense que oui;** I'll think about it **je vais y penser**
third **troisième**
thirsty: I'm thirsty **j'ai soif**
thirteen **treize**
thirty **trente**
this (this one) **ceci;** this bus **ce bus;** this man **cet homme;** this woman **cette femme;** what's this? **qu'est-ce que c'est?;** this is Mr.... **je vous présente M....**
those: those things **ces choses-là;** those are his **ils/elles sont à lui**
thousand **mille**
three **trois**
throat **la gorge**
throat lozenges **les pastilles pour la gorge** (f)
through **à travers**
thumbtack **la punaise**
thunderstorm **l'orage** (m)
Thursday **jeudi**
ticket **le billet;** (underground, bus) **le ticket**
ticket collector **le/la contrôleur(euse)**
ticket office **le guichet**
tide **la marée**

tie **la cravate;** (verb) **nouer**
tight (adj) **étroit(e)**
tights **les collants** (m)
tiles, tiling **le carrelage**
time **l'heure** (f); what's the time? **quelle heure est-il?**
timetable (train, bus) **l'horaire** (f)
tip (money) **le pourboire;** (end) **le bout**
tire **le pneu**
tired (adj) **fatigué(e)**
tissues **les mouchoirs** (m)
to: to England **en Angleterre;** to Paris **à Paris;** to the station **à la gare;** to the center **au centre;** to the doctor **chez le docteur**
toast **le pain grillé**
tobacco **le tabac**
tobacconist **le tabac**
toboggan **le toboggan**
today **aujourd'hui**
together **ensemble**
toilet paper **le papier hygiénique**
toilets **les toilettes** (f)
tomato **la tomate**
tomorrow **demain;** see you tomorrow **à demain**
tongue **la langue**
tonic **le tonic**
tonight **ce soir**
too (also) **aussi;** (excessively) **trop**
tooth **la dent**
toothache **le mal de dents**
toothbrush **la brosse à dents**
toothpaste **le dentifrice**
torch **la lampe de poche**
tour **la visite**
tourist **le/la touriste**
tourist office **l'office de tourisme** (m)
towel **la serviette**
tower **la tour**
town **la ville**
town center **le centre-ville**
town hall **l'hôtel de ville** (m); **la mairie**
toy **le jouet**
tracksuit **le survêtement**
tractor **le tracteur**
trade fair **la foire**
tradition **la tradition**
traffic **la circulation, le trafic**
traffic laws **le code de la route**

traffic lights **les feux** (m)
trailer **la remorque**
train **le train**
trainee **le/la stagiaire**
translate (verb) **traduire**
translator **le/la traducteur(trice)**
transmission **la boîte de vitesses**
trash can **la poubelle**
trash can liner **le sac poubelle**
travel agency **l'agence de voyages** (f)
tray **le plateau**
tree **l'arbre** (m)
trolley **le chariot**
trousers **le pantalon**
truck **le camion**
true **vrai(e)**
try (verb) **essayer**
Tuesday **mardi**
tunnel **le tunnel**
tweezers **la pince à épiler**
twelve **douze**
twenty **vingt**
two **deux**

U

ugly (adj) **laid(e)**
umbrella **le parapluie**
uncle **l'oncle** (m)
under **sous**
underground **le métro**
underpants **le slip**
understand (verb) **comprendre;** I understand **je comprends;** I don't understand **je ne comprends pas**
underwear **le sous-vêtement**
university **l'université** (f)
university lecturer **le/la maître(resse) de conférences**
unleaded **sans plomb**
until **jusqu'à**
unusual (adj) **inhabituel(le)**
up **en haut;** (upward) **vers le haut;** up there **là-haut**
urgent (adj) **urgent(e)**
us: it's us **c'est nous;** it's for us **c'est pour nous;** give it to us **donnez-le-nous**
use (verb) **utiliser;** it's no use **ça ne sert à rien**
useful (adj) **utile**
usual (adj) **habituel(le)**
usually **d'habitude**

V

vacancy (room) **la chambre de libre**
vaccinate (verb) **vacciner**
vaccination **la vaccination**
vaccine **le vaccin**
vacuum cleaner **l'aspirateur** (m)
valley **la vallée**
valve **la soupape**
vanilla **la vanille**
vase **le vase**
VCR **le magnétoscope**
veal **le veau**
vegetables **les légumes** (m)
vegetarian (adj) **végétarien(ne)**
vehicle **le véhicule**
very **très;** very much **beaucoup**
vet **le/la vétérinaire**
video (film/tape) **la vidéo**
video games **les jeux vidéos** (m)
view **la vue**
viewfinder **le viseur**
villa **la villa**
village **le village**
vinegar **le vinaigre**
violin **le violon**
visit **la visite;** (verb: place) **visiter;** (verb: person) **rendre visite**
visitor **le/la visiteur(euse)**
vitamin pill **le comprimé de vitamines**
vodka **la vodka**
voice **la voix**
voicemail **la messagerie téléphonique**

W

wait (verb) **attendre;** wait! **attendez!**
waiter **le serveur;** waiter! **monsieur!**
waiting room **la salle d'attente**
waitress **la serveuse;** waitress! **madame!**
Wales **le pays de Galles**
walk (verb) **marcher;** to go for a walk **aller se promener**
wall (inside) **la paroi;** (outside) **le mur**
wallet **le portefeuille**
want (verb) **vouloir;** I would like **je voudrais**
war **la guerre**
wardrobe **l'armoire** (f)

warm (adj) **chaud(e)**
was: I was **j'étais;** he was **il était;** she was **elle était;** it was **il/elle était**
washer **la rondelle**
washing machine **la machine à laver**
wasp **la guêpe**
watch **la montre;** (verb) **regarder**
water **l'eau** (f)
waterfall **la chute d'eau**
water heater **le chauffe-eau**
wave **la vague;** (verb) **faire signe de la main**
wavy (adj: hair) **ondulé(e)**
we **nous**
weather **le temps**
website **le site web**
wedding **le mariage**
Wednesday **mercredi**
weeds **les mauvaises herbes** (f)
week **la semaine**
welcome: you're welcome **je vous en prie**
were: we were **nous étions;** you were **vous étiez;** they were **ils/elles étaient**
west **l'ouest**
wet (adj) **mouillé(e)**
what? **comment?;** what is it? **qu'est-ce que c'est?**
wheel **la roue**
wheelchair **le fauteuil roulant; la chaise roulante**
when? **quand?**
where? **où?**
whether **si**
which? **lequel?,** (fem) **laquelle?**
whisky **le whisky**
white **blanc,** (fem) **blanche**
who? **qui?**
why? **pourquoi?**
wide (adj) **large**
wife **la femme**
wind **le vent**
window **la fenêtre**
windscreen **le pare-brise**
wine **le vin**
wine list **la carte des vins**
wine merchant **le/la négociant(e) en vins**
wing **l'aile** (f)
winter **l'hiver** (m)
with **avec;** with pleasure **avec plaisir**
withdraw (verb) **retirer**
without **sans**
witness **le/la témoin**
woman **la femme**
wood **le bois**

wool **la laine**
word **le mot**
work **le travail;** (verb: person) **travailler;** (verb: machine, etc.) **fonctionner**
worktop **le plan de travail**
worse **pire**
worst **le pire**
wrapping paper **le papier d'emballage;** (for presents) **le papier cadeau**
wrench **la clé**
wrist **le poignet**
write (verb) **écrire;** written by **écrit par**
writing paper **le papier à lettres**
wrong (adj) **faux,** (fem) **fausse**

X, Y, Z

x-ray **la radio**
x-ray department **le service de radiologie**
year **l'an** (m); **l'année** (f)
yellow **jaune** (m/f)
yes **oui**
yesterday **hier**
yet **déjà;** not yet **pas encore**
yogurt **le yaourt**
you (singular informal) **tu;** (plural; singular formal) **vous**
young (adj) **jeune** (m/f)
your (singular informal): your book **ton livre;** your house **ta maison;** your shoes **tes chaussures;** it's yours **c'est à toi;** (singular formal; plural): your house **votre maison;** your shoes **vos chaussures;** it's yours **c'est à vous**
youth hostel **l'auberge de jeunesse** (f)
zip **la fermeture éclair**
zip code **le code postal**
zoo **le zoo**
zucchini **la courgette**

Dictionary
FRENCH TO ENGLISH

The gender of French nouns listed here is indicated by the abbreviations (m) and (f), for masculine and feminine. Plural nouns are indicated by (m pl) or (f pl). French adjectives (adj) vary according to the gender and number of the word they describe; the masculine form is shown here. In most cases, you add an **-e** to the masculine form to make it feminine. Certain endings use a different rule: masculine adjectives that end in **-x** adopt an **-se** ending in the feminine form, while those that end in **-ien** change to **-ienne**. Some feminine adjectives that do not follow these rules are shown here and follow the abbreviation (fem). For the plural form, a (silent) **-s** is usually added.

A

à: *at:* **à la poste** *at the post office;* **à trois heures** *at 3 o'clock;* **à côté de** *beside;* **à demain** *see you tomorrow;* **à emporter** *to take away;* **à travers** *through*
abat-jour (m) *lampshade*
abricot (m) *apricot*
accélérateur (m) *accelerator*
accident (m) *accident*
acheter (verb) *to buy*
adaptateur (m) *adaptor* (voltage)
addition (f) *bill*
adhésif (m) *adhesive*
adresse (f) *address*
adresse électronique (f) *email address*
aéroglisseur (m) *hovercraft*
aéroport (m) *airport*
affaire (f) *bargain*
affaires (f pl) *business*
affiche (f) *poster* (outside)
affreux(euse) (adj) *awful*
agence de voyages (f) *travel agency*
agenda (m) *diary*
agent(e) *agent*
agneau (m) *lamb*
agrafeuse (f) *stapler*
agrandissement (m) *enlargement*
aide (f) *help*
aider (verb) *to help*
aiguille (f) *needle;* **aiguille à tricoter** (f) *knitting needle*
ail (m) *garlic*
aile (f) *wing*
ailleurs *somewhere else*
aimer *to like/love;* **j'aime nager** *I like swimming;* **je n'aime pas** *I don't like*
air (m) *air*

alcool (m) *alcohol*
Algérie (f) *Algeria*
algérien(ne) *Algerian*
allée (f) *path, driveway*
Allemagne (f) *Germany*
allemand(e) *German*
aller (verb) *to go*
aller chercher (verb) *to get* (fetch)
allergique *allergic*
aller patiner (verb) *to go ice-skating*
aller retour (m) *return ticket*
aller simple (m) *single ticket*
allez-vous en! *go away!*
allumage (m) *ignition*
allumette (f) *match* (light)
alors *well then*
Alpes: les Alpes (m pl) *Alps*
amant (m) *lover*
ambassade (f) *embassy*
ambulance (f) *ambulance*
amer, (fem) amère (adj) *bitter*
américain(e) *American*
Amérique (f) *America*
ami(e) *friend*
amical(e) *friendly*
amour (m) *love*
amphithéâtre (m) *lecture hall*
ampoule (f) *blister; light bulb*
an (m) *year*
analyse de sang (f) *blood test*
ananas (m) *pineapple*
Andorre (f) *Andorra*
anglais(e) *English*
Angleterre (f) *England*
animaux (familiers) (m pl) *pets*
animé(e) *busy* (street)
année (f) *year*
anniversaire (m) *birthday*
annuaire (m) *directory* (telephone)

antigel (m) *antifreeze*
antiseptique (m) *antiseptic*
août *August*
apéritif (m) *aperitif*
appareil auditif (m) *hearing aid*
appareil-photo (m) *camera*
appartement (m) *apartment*
appât (m) *bait*
appétit (m) *appetite*
apprendre (verb) *to learn*
après *after*
après-midi (m) *afternoon*
après-rasage (m) *aftershave*
après-shampooing (m) *conditioner* (hair)
araignée (f) *spider*
arbre (m) *tree*
arbre à cames (m) *camshaft*
architecture (f) *architecture*
arête (f) *fishbone*
argent (m) *cash, money; silver* (metal)
argent(e) *silver* (color)
armoire (f) *wardrobe*
arrêt de bus (m) *bus stop*
arrière (m) *back* (not front)
arrivée (f) *arrival*
arriver (verb) *to arrive*
art (m) *art*
artiste (m/f) *artist*
ascenseur (m) *lift*
aspirateur (m) *vacuum cleaner*
aspirine (f) *aspirin*
assez *enough; fairly*
assiette (f) *plate*
assurance (f) *insurance*
asthmatique *asthmatic*
attaché-case (m) *briefcase*
attendez! *wait!*
attendre (verb) *to wait*
attention! *careful!*
atterrir (verb) *to land*

attirant(e) (adj) *attractive*
au: au café *at the café;*
  au revoir *goodbye*
auberge (f) *inn*
auberge de jeunesse (f)
  youth hostel
aucun(e) *not any; none*
audioguide (m) *audio guide*
au-dessus de *over (above)*
aujourd'hui *today*
aussi *too (also)*
Australie (f) *Australia*
australien(ne) *Australian*
automatique *automatic*
automne (m) *autumn*
autoroute (f) *motorway*
autre: autre chose
  something else
avance (f) *advance*
avant *before*
avec *with;* **avec plaisir**
  with pleasure
averse (f) *shower (rain)*
aveugle (adj) *blind*
  (cannot see)
avion (m) *aircraft*
avocat (m) *avocado*
avocat(e) *lawyer*
avoir (verb) *to have*
avril *April*

B

bac (m) *ferry (small)*
bagages (m pl) *luggage;*
  baggage; **bagages à main**
  (m pl) *hand luggage*
baigner: aller se
  baigner (verb) *to*
  go swimming
bain (m) *bath*
balai (m) *broom*
balcon (m) *balcony*
balle (f) *ball (tennis, etc.)*
ballon (m) *ball (football, etc.)*
banane (f) *banana*
bandage (m) *bandage*
banlieue (f) *suburbs*
banque (f) *bank*
bar (m) *bar (place)*
barbe (f) *beard*
barbecue (m) *barbecue*
barque (f) *rowing boat*
bas (m) *stockings;* **bas(se)**
  (adj) *low;* **en bas** *down*
bateau (m) *boat; ship;*
bateau à moteur (m)
  motorboat; **bateau à**
  vapeur (m) *steamer*
bâtiment (m) *building*
bâton de ski (m) *ski pole*
batterie (f) *battery (car)*
beau, (fem) **belle** (adj)
  beautiful

bébé (m) *baby*
bêche (f) *spade (garden)*
beige *beige*
beignet (m) *doughnut*
belge *Belgian*
Belgique: la Belgique *Belgium*
bénéfices (m pl) *profits*
béquilles (f pl) *crutches*
besoin: avoir besoin de
  to need; **j'ai besoin de...**
  I need...
beurre (m) *butter*
bibliothèque (f) *library*
bicyclette (f) *bicycle*
bien sûr *of course*
bien! *good!;* **ça vous va bien**
  it suits you
bière (f) *beer*
bijouterie (f) *jeweler's*
billet (m) *ticket; paper money*
billetterie (f) *box office*
biscuit (m) *biscuit*
blanc, (fem) **blanche** *white*
blanchisserie (f) *laundry*
  (place)
blême (adj) *pale*
blessure (f) *injury*
bleu (m) *bruise;* **bleu(e)**
  (adj) *blue*
bloc notes (m) *notepad*
blond(e) (adj) *blond*
bœuf (m) *beef*
boire (verb) *to drink;* **vous**
  voulez boire quelque
  chose? *would you like*
  something to drink?
bois (m) *wood*
boisson (f) *drink*
boîte (f) *box;* **boîte aux**
lettres *mailbox;* **boîte de**
  chocolats *box of*
  chocolates; **boîte de**
  conserve *can (vessel);*
  boîte de nuit *nightclub;*
  boîte de vitesses *gearbox*
  bottes en caoutchouc
  (f pl) *rubber boots*
bol (m) *bowl*
bon, (fem) **bonne** *good*
bonbon (m) *sweet*
  (confectionery); **bonbons**
  à la menthe (m pl)
  peppermints
bondé(e) (adj) *crowded*
bonjour *hello*
bon marché (adj)
  inexpensive; cheap
bonne chance! *good luck!*
bonsoir *good evening*
bord (m) *side (edge)*
borne de recharge (f)
  charging point/station
botte (f) *boot (footwear)*
bouche (f) *mouth*

boucherie (f) *butcher's*
bouchon (m) *plug (sink);* **cork**
boucles (f pl) *curls*
boucles d'oreille (f pl)
  earrings
boucles magnétiques (f pl)
  hearing loop
bouger (adj) *to move;*
  ne bougez pas!
  don't move!
bougie (f) *spark plug; candle*
bouilli(e) (adj) *boiled*
bouillir (verb) *to boil*
bouilloire (f) *kettle*
boulangerie (f) *bakery*
bout (m) *tip, end*
bouteille (f) *bottle*
bouton (m) *button;* **boutons**
  de manchette (m pl)
  cuff links
bracelet (m) *bracelet*
branche (f) *branch*
bras (m) *arm*
Bretagne: la Bretagne
  Brittany
bretelles (f pl) *braces*
  (clothes)
briquet (m) *lighter*
britannique *British*
broche (f) *brooch*
brochure (f) *brochure*
broderie (f) *embroidery*
bronzage (m) *suntan*
bronzer: se faire bronzer
  (verb) *to sunbathe*
brosse (f) *brush;*
  brosse à dents (f)
  toothbrush
brosser (verb) *to brush*
brouillard (m) *fog*
brûler (verb) *to burn*
brûlure (f) *burn*
Bruxelles *Brussels*
bruyant(e) (adj) *noisy*
budget (m) *budget*
bunker (m) *bunker*
bureau (m) *desk; office*
bureau de change (m)
  bureau de change
bus (m) *bus*

C

ça *that (that one)*
cabine téléphonique (f)
  telephone box
câble de recharge (m)
  charging cable
cacahuètes (f pl) *peanuts*
cachet (m) *tablet*
cadeau (m) *gift*
cadenas (m) *padlock*
cadre (m/f) *executive*
  (in company)

cafard (m) *cockroach*
café (m) *café; coffee;* **café crème** *coffee with milk;* **café soluble** *instant coffee*
cage (f) *cage*
caisse (f) *checkout (supermarket)*
calculette (f) *calculator*
cambriolage (m) *burglary*
caméscope (m) *camcorder*
camion (m) *truck*
campagne (f) *countryside*
camping (m) *campsite*
camping-car (m) *camper van*
Canada (m) *Canada*
canadien(ne) *Canadian*
canal (m) *canal*
canif (m) *penknife*
canne à pêche (f) *fishing rod*
canoë (m) *canoe*
caoutchouc (m) *rubber (material)*
capot (m) *car hood*
capsule (f) *cap (bottle)*
caravane (f) *caravan*
carburateur (m) *carburetor*
carnet (m) *notebook;* **carnet de chèques** (m) *checkbook*
carotte (f) *carrot*
carré(e) (adj: shape) *square*
carreau (m) *diamonds (cards)*
carrelage (m) *tiles, tiling*
carte (f) *menu; card; map;* **carte bancaire** *debit card;* **carte de crédit** *credit card;* **carte d'embarquement** *boarding pass;* **carte des vins** *wine list;* **carte de visite** *business card;* **carte postale** *postcard;* **carte téléphonique** *phone card;* **carte en ligne** *online map*
casque (m) *headphones*
casquette (f) *cap (hat)*
cassé(e) (adj) *broken*
casserole (f) *saucepan*
cassette (f) *cassette*
cassis (m) *black currant*
cathédrale (f) *cathedral*
caution (f) *deposit*
cave (f) *cellar*
ce (bus) *that (bus)*
ceci *this (this one)*
ceinture (f) *belt;* **ceinture de sécurité** *seat belt*
célibataire (adj) *single (unmarried)*

cellule photoélectrique (f) *light meter*
cendrier (m) *ashtray*
cent *hundred*
centre (m) *center;* **centre sportif** (m) *sports center* **centre-ville** (m) *town center*
cerise (f) *cherry*
certificat (m) *certificate*
ces (choses) *these (things)*
c'est *it's;* **c'est tout** *that's all*
cet (homme) *that (man)*
cette (femme) *that (woman)*
chaise (f) *chair*
châle (m) *shawl*
chambre (f) *bedroom;* **chambre de libre** *vacancy;* **chambre pour deux personnes** *double room;* **chambre simple** *single room*
chambre à air (f) *inner tube*
champ (m) *field (farming)*
champignon (m) *mushroom*
chance (f) *luck*
changer (verb) *to change (money);* **se changer** (verb) *to change (clothes)*
chanson (f) *song*
chanter (verb) *to sing*
chapeau (m) *hat*
chaque *each; every*
charcuterie (f) *delicatessen*
chargeur (m) *cell phone charger*
chariot (m) *trolley*
charpentier(ière) *carpenter*
chat (m) *cat*
château (m) *castle*
chaud(e) (adj) *hot; warm;* **j'ai chaud** *I feel hot*
chauffage (m) *heating;* **chauffage central** *central heating*
chauffe-eau (m) *boiler; water heater*
chaussettes (f pl) *socks*
chaussures (f pl) *shoes;* **chaussures de ski** (f pl) *ski boots*
chauve (adj) *bald*
chef(fe) *manager;* **chef(fe) d'orchestre** *conductor (orchestra);* **chef(fe) de train** *guard (train)*
chemin (m) *path*
chemin de fer (m) *railway*
cheminée (f) *fireplace; chimney*
chemise (f) *shirt;* **chemise de nuit** *nightdress*

chemisier (m) *blouse*
chèque (m) *check;*
cher (fem) **chère** (adj) *dear; expensive;* **pas cher** *inexpensive*
cheveux (m pl) *hair;* **les cheveux longs/courts** *long/short hair*
cheville (f) *ankle*
chez *at home;* **chez moi;** *at my house;* **chez vous** *at your place*
chien (m) *dog*
chiffon à poussière (m) *duster*
chiffres (m pl) *figures*
chips (f pl) *chips*
chocolat (m) *chocolate*
chou (m) *cabbage*
chou-fleur (m) *cauliflower*
chute d'eau (f) *waterfall*
ciel (m) *sky*
cigare (m) *cigar*
cigarette (f) *cigarette*
cimetière (m) *cemetery*
cinéma (m) *movie theater*
cinq *five*
cinquante *fifty*
cintre (m) *coat hanger*
cirage (m) *shoe polish*
circulation (f) *traffic*
ciseaux (m pl) *scissors*
citron (m) *lemon;* **citron vert** *lime*
clair(e) (adj) *clear; light (not dark)*
classe (f) *class*
clavier (m) *keyboard*
clé (f) *key; wrench*
clignotant (m) *indicator*
climatisation (f) *air conditioning*
cloche (f) *bell (church)*
clou (m) *nail (metal)*
cocktail (m) *cocktail party*
code (m) *PIN*
code de la route (m) *traffic laws*
code postal (m) *zip code*
cœur (m) *heart;* **cœurs** (m pl) *hearts (cards);* **problème cardiaque** *heart condition*
coffre (m) *boot (car)*
cognac (m) *brandy*
coiffeur(euse) (m) *hairdresser; barber's*
coin (m) *corner*
col (m) *collar*
colis (m) *parcel*
collants (m pl) *tights*
colle (f) *glue*
collection (f) *collection (stamps, etc.)*

collier (m) *collar; necklace*
colline (f) *hill*
combien? *how much?;*
  combien ça coûte? *how much does it cost?*
comme *like (similar to)*
commencer (verb) *to start*
comment? *how?;* **comment allez-vous?** *how are you?;* **comment est-ce que ça s'appelle?** *what's it called?;* **comment vous appelez-vous?** *what's your name?*
commerçant(e) *shopkeeper*
commissariat (m) *police station*
commode (f) *chest of drawers*
compagnie *company*
compagnie aérienne *airline*
compartiment (m) *compartment*
complet *full*
compliqué(e) (adj) *complicated*
comprendre (verb) *to understand;* **je comprends** *I understand;* **je ne comprends pas** *I don't understand*
comprimé (m) *pill;* **comprimé de vitamines** *vitamin pill*
comptable (m/f) *accountant*
compte: à mon compte *self-employed*
concert (m) *concert*
concierge (m/f) *caretaker*
concombre (m) *cucumber*
conducteur(trice) *driver*
conduire (verb) *to drive*
conférence (f) *conference*
confiseur (m) *confectioner*
confiture (f) *jam*
congélateur (m) *freezer*
connaître (verb) *to know (person)*
consigne automatique (f) *luggage lockers*
constructeur(trice) *builder*
consulat (m) *consulate*
consultant(e) *consultant*
contraceptif (m) *contraceptive*
contre *against*
contrôle des passeports (m) *passport control*
contrôleur(euse) *ticket collector*
conversation (f) *talk*
copieur (m) *photocopier*

coquille (f) *shell*
corde (f) *rope; string (guitar, etc.)*
cordonnerie (f) *shoemaker*
corne (f) *horn* (animal)
corps (m) *body*
correspondant(e) *pen pal*
corse *Corsican*
Corse: la Corse *Corsica*
costume (m) *suit*
côtelette (f) *chop (food)*
coton (m) *cotton;* **coton hydrophile** *cotton balls*
cou (m) *neck*
couche (f) *diaper;* **couches à jeter** (f pl) *disposable diapers*
coude (m) *elbow*
coudre (verb) *to sew*
couette (f) *duvet*
couleur (f) *color*
couloir (m) *corridor*
coup de soleil (m) *sunburn*
coupe (de cheveux) (f) *haircut*
couper (verb) *to cut, chop*
coupure (f) *cut*
courant(e) *current*
courgette (f) *zucchiniss*
courir (verb) *to run*
courroie du ventilateur (f) *fan belt*
courses (f pl) *shopping;* **faire les courses** (verb) *to go shopping*
court(e) *short*
coussoussier (m) *steamer (cooking)*
cousin(e) *cousin*
couteau (m) *knife*
coûter (verb) *to cost*
couverture (f) *blanket; rug*
crabe (m) *crab*
crampe (f) *cramp*
cravate (f) *tie*
crayon (m) *pencil*
crème (f) *cream;* **crème anti-insecte** (f) *insect repellent cream*
crêpe (f) *pancake*
crevaison (f) *puncture*
crevette (f) *shrimp*
crier (verb) *to cry (shout)*
croisière (f) *cruise*
crustacés (m) *shellfish*
cuillère (f) *spoon*
cuir (m) *leather*
cuire (verb) *to bake*
cuisine (f) *kitchen*
cuisinier(ière) *cook*
cuisinière (f) *cooker*
curry (m) *curry*

D

d'accord *OK*
danger (m) *danger;* **dangereux(euse)** (adj) *dangerous;* **sans danger** (adj) *safe*
dans *in*
danse (f) *dance*
danser (verb) *to dance*
de *of*
début (m) *start (beginning)*
débutant(e) *beginner*
décapsuleur (m) *bottle opener*
décembre *December*
décollage (m) *takeoff*
décolorer (verb) *to bleach*
décorateur(trice) *decorator*
dehors *outside*
déjà *yet; already*
déjeuner (m) *lunch*
delco (m) *distributor (car)*
demain *tomorrow*
démaquillant (m) *skin cleanser*
déménager *to move house*
demi *half;* **une demi-heure** *half an hour*
demi-pension (f) *half board*
dent (f) *tooth*
dentelle (f) *lace*
dentier (m) *dentures*
dentifrice (m) *toothpaste*
dentiste (m/f) *dentist*
déodorant (m) *deodorant*
départs (m pl) *departures*
département (f) *department*
dépliant (m) *leaflet*
déposition (f) *statement*
déraper (verb) *to skid*
dernier(ière) *last (final);* **la semaine dernière** *last week*
derrière *behind*
descendre (verb) *to get off (bus, etc.)*
designer (m/f) *designer*
désinfectant pour les mains *hand sanitizer*
désolé: je suis désolé(e) *I'm sorry*
desserts (m pl) *desserts*
déteste *hate*
détritus (m) *trash*
deux *two;* **les deux** *both*
deuxième *second (in series)*
devant *in front of*
développer (verb) *to develop*
devis (m) *quotation*

d'habitude usually
diabétique diabetic
diamant (m) diamond (jewel)
diarrhée (f) diarrhea
dictionnaire (m) dictionary
diesel (m) diesel
différent(e) (adj) different;
   c'est différent that's
   different
difficile (adj) difficult
dimanche Sunday
dîner (m) dinner
dire to say; **qu'avez-vous
   dit?** what did you say?;
   comment dit-on...? how
   do you say...?; **qu'est-ce
   que cela veut dire?** what
   does this mean?
directeur(trice) director
discothèque (f) disco
disquaire (m/f) record seller
disque (m) record (music);
   disque compact (m)
   compact disc
distributeur automatique
   (m) ATM
divertissement (m)
   entertainment
divorcé(e) (adj) divorced
dix ten
dix-huit eighteen
dix-neuf nineteen
dix-sept seventeen
docteur (m) doctor
document (m) document
doigt (m) finger
dois: je dois... I must...
dollar (m) dollar
domaine (m) field (academic)
donner give
dormir (verb) to sleep
dos (m) back (body)
douane (f) customs
doubler (verb) to overtake
   (in a car)
douche (f) shower (bath)
douleur (f) ache; pain
douze twelve
drap (m) sheet
drapeau (m) flag
draps (m pl) bed linen
droit (m) law
droite right (not left)
drôle (adj) funny
dunes (f pl) sand dunes
dur(e) (adj) hard

E

eau (f) water; **eau gazeuse**
   fizzy water; **eau minérale**
   mineral water; **eau potable**
   drinking water; **eau de
   Javel** bleach

échanger (verb) to exchange
écharpe (f) scarf
échecs (m pl) chess
école (f) school
Écosse: l'Écosse (f) Scotland
écouteurs (m) earphones
écran (m) screen
écrevisse (f) crayfish
   (freshwater)
écrire (verb) to write; **écrit
   par...** written by...
écrou (m) nut (for bolt)
église (f) church
élastique (m) rubber band;
   (adj) elastic
électricien(ne) electrician
électricité (f) electricity
électrique electric
elle she
elles they (f pl)
email (m) email
embrayage (m) clutch
émeraude (f) emerald
emplacement (m) pitch
emploi du temps (m) schedule
employé(e) de ménage
   cleaning staff
en in; **en France** in France
enchanté(e) pleased to
   meet you
encore: encore un café
   another coffee
encre (f) ink
endormi(e) asleep
endroit (m) place
enfant (m) child
enfin! at last!
ennuyeux(euse) (adj)
   boring
enregistrement (m)
   check-in; **enregistrement
   des bagages** baggage
   check-in
ensemble together
ensoleillé(e) (adj) sunny
ensuite then (after)
entendre hear
entre... between...
entrée (f) entrance
entrées (f pl) starters
entreprise (f) company
enveloppe (f) envelope
envie: j'ai envie de...
   I feel like...
environ about
envoyer (verb) to send
épais(se) (adj) thick
épaule (f) shoulder
épicerie (f) grocery
épileptique epileptic
épinards (m) spinach
épingle (f) pin; **épingle à
   nourrice** safety pin
erreur (f) mistake

escalier (m) stairs; staircase;
   escalier roulant escalator
Espagne: l'Espagne (f) Spain
espagnol(e) Spanish
essayer (verb) to try
essence (f) gasoline
essieu (m) axle
est (m) east
est is; **il/elle est** he/she is;
   c'est it is
estimation (f) estimate
estomac (m) stomach
espèces (f pl) cash
et and
étage (m) floor (storey)
été (m) summer
étiquette (f) label
étoile (f) star
étouffant(e) close (stuffy)
étranger(ère) foreigner
être (verb) to be
étroit(e) (adj) narrow; tight
étudiant(e) student
eux: c'est à eux it's theirs;
   c'est pour eux/elles it's
   for them
evanouir (verb) to faint
évier (m) sink
excédent de bagages (m)
   excess baggage
excellent(e) excellent
excursion (f) excursion
exemple (m) example
exposition (f) exhibition
exprès deliberately
extérieur (m) exterior;
   (adj) **extérieur(e)**
extincteur (m) fire
   extinguisher

F

face: en face de
   opposite
facile (adj) easy
**façon: d'une façon ou
   d'une autre** somehow
facteur(trice) postman
facture (f) invoice
faim: j'ai faim I'm hungry
faire (verb) to do; make;
   faire de autostop to
   hitchhike; **faire du
   jogging** to jog; **faire
   enregistrer ses bagages**
   to check in; **faire la
   cuisine** to cook; **faire
   la queue** to queue; **faire
   signe de la
   main** to wave
fan (m/f) fan (enthusiast)
fantastique fantastic
farine (f) flour
fatigué(e) (adj) tired

fauteuil (m) *armchair;*
  fauteuil roulant (m)
  wheelchair
faux, (fem) **fausse**
  (adj) *wrong*
félicitations! *congratulations!*
femme (f) *woman; wife*
fenêtre (f) *window*
fer à repasser (m) *iron*
  (for clothes)
ferme (f) *farm*
fermé(e) (adj) *closed*
fermer (verb) *to close*
fermeture éclair (f) *zip*
fermier(ière) *farmer*
ferry (m) *ferry* (large)
fête (f) *party* (celebration)
feu (m) *fire;* **feu d'artifice**
  fireworks; **feu de camp**
  campfire
feuille (f) *leaf*
feutre (m) *felt-tip pen*
feux (m pl) *lights; traffic*
  lights; **feux de position**
  (m pl) *sidelights*
fevrier *February*
fiancé *engaged* (couple)
fiancé(e) *fiancé(e)*
ficelle (f) *string* (cord)
fièvre (f) *fever*
figue (f) *fig*
fille (f) *girl; daughter*
film (m) *film*
fils (m) *son*
fin (f) *end*
fini(e) *over* (finished)
flash (m) *flash* (camera)
fleur (f) *flower*
fleuriste (m/f) *florist*
fleuve (m) *river* (big)
flûte (f) *flute*
foie (m) *liver*
foire (f) *fair; trade fair*
foncé(e) (adj) *dark;* **bleu**
  foncé *dark blue*
fonctionner *function*
  (machine, etc.)
fond (m) *bottom*
football (m) *soccer;* **les**
  chaussures de football
  (f pl) *soccer cleats*
forêt (f) *forest*
formulaire de
  demande (m)
  application form
fort(e) *loud; strong*
  (person, drink)
fou, (fem) **folle** (adj) *mad*
foulard (m) *headscarf*
four (m) *oven*
fourchette (f) *fork*
frais, (fem) **fraîche** (adj) *cool*
fraise (f) *strawberry*
framboise (f) *raspberry*

français(e) *French*
France: la France *France*
frange (f) *fringe*
frein (m) *brake;* **frein à main**
  handbrake
freiner (verb) *to brake*
frère (m) *brother*
frigo (m) *fridge*
frire (verb) *to fry*
frit (adj) *fried*
frites (f pl) *French fries*
froid(e) (adj) *cold*
fromage (m) *cheese*
fromagerie (f) *cheese shop*
frontière (f) *border*
fruit (m) *fruit*
fruits de mer (m pl) *seafood*
fumée (f) *smoke*
fumer (verb) *to smoke*
fusil (m) *rifle*

G

galerie d'art (f) *art gallery*
gamelle (f) *animal's bowl*
gants (m pl) *gloves*
garage (m) *garage*
garagiste (m/f) *mechanic*
garantie (f) *guarantee*
garantir (verb) *to guarantee*
garçon (m) *boy*
gare (f) *station;* **gare**
  routière (f) *bus station*
garer (verb) *to park*
garniture (f) *filling*
  (in sandwich, cake)
gâteau (m) *cake*
gauche *left* (not right)
gaz (m) *gas;* **gaz à briquet**
  (m) *lighter fluid*
gazole (m) *diesel*
gel (m) *gel; frost;* **gel**
  douche (m) *shower gel*
gênant (adj) *embarrassing*
genou (m) *knee*
gens (m pl) *people*
gentil(le) *friendly; kind*
gilet (m) *cardigan*
gin (m) *gin*
gingembre (m) *ginger*
glace (f) *ice; ice cream*
golf (m) *golf*
gomme (f) *eraser*
gorge (f) *throat*
goût (m) *flavor*
goutes (f pl) *drops*
gouttière (f) *gutter*
gouvernement (m)
  government
grand(e) (adj) *big; large; tall;*
  grand magasin (m)
  department store
Grande-Bretagne (f)
  Great Britain

grand-mère (f) *grandmother*
grand-père (m) *grandfather*
grands-parents (m pl)
  grandparents
gras(se) *fat* (on
  meat, etc.)
gratuit(e) *free* (of charge)
grenier (m) *attic*
gril (m) *grill*
grillé(e) (adj) *grilled*
gris(e) *grey*
gros, (fem) **grosse** (adj) *fat*
grotte (f) *cave*
groupe (m) *group; band*
  (musicians)
guêpe (f) *wasp*
guerre (f) *war*
gueule de bois (f) *hangover*
guichet (m) *cashier; ticket*
  office; box office
guide (m) *guide; guidebook;*
  guide de conversation
  (m) *phrase book*
guitare (f) *guitar*

H

habituel(le) (adj)
  ordinary; usual
hache (f) *ax*
haie (f) *hedge*
hamburger (m) *hamburger*
hamster (m) *hamster*
handicapé(e) *disabled*
haricots (m pl) *beans*
haut(e) *high;* **en haut** *up;*
  vers la haut *upward;*
  là-haut *up there*
hébergement (m)
  accommodation
hépatite (f) *hepatitis*
herbe (f) *grass*
heure (f) *hour; time*
heures d'ouverture
  (f pl) *opening times*
heureux(euse) (adj)
  glad; happy
hier *yesterday*
histoire (f) *history*
hiver (m) *winter*
homard (m) *lobster*
homéopathie *homeopathy*
homme (m) *man*
homosexuel(le) *gay*
honnête (adj) *honest*
hôpital (m) *hospital*
horaire (m) *timetable*
  (train, bus)
horloge (f) *clock;*
  horloge de bureau (f)
  desk clock; **horloge**
  murale (f) *wall clock*
horrible (adj) *horrible*
hors-taxe *duty-free*

hôte (m) *host*
hôtel (m) *hotel*
hôtel de ville (m) *town hall*
hôtesse(f) *hostess;* **hôtesse de air** *flight attendant*
hoverport (m) *hoverport*
huile (f) *oil*
huit *eight*
huître (f) *oyster*
hydrofoil (m) *hydrofoil*

I

il *he; it* (m)
île (f) *island;* **les îles Anglo-Normandes** *Channel Islands*
ils *they* (m)**; ils sont** *they are*
il y a... *there is/are...*
immédiatement *immediately*
imperméable (m) *raincoat*
impossible *impossible*
imprimante (f) *printer*
incendie (m) *fire* (blaze)
indigestion (f) *indigestion*
infection (f) *infection*
infirmier(ière) *nurse*
information (f) *information*
informations (f pl) *news* (TV)
ingénierie (f) *engineering*
ingénieur(e) *engineer*
inhabituel(le) (adj) *unusual*
insecte (m) *insect*
insomnie (f) *insomnia*
instrument de musique (m) *musical instrument*
intelligent(e) (adj) *clever*
intéressant(e) (adj) *interesting*
internet (m) *Internet*
interprète (m) *interpreter*
interpréter (verb) *to interpret*
interrupteur (m) *switch*
intoxication alimentaire (f) *food poisoning*
invitation (f) *invitation*
invité(e) *guest*
irlandais(e) *Irish*
Irlande (f) *Ireland*
Italie (f) *Italy*
italien(ne) *Italian*
ivre (adj) *drunk*

J

jamais *never*
jambe (f) *leg;* **jambe cassée** (f) *broken leg*
jambon (m) *ham*
janvier *January*
jardin (m) *garden;* **jardin public** (m) *park*
jardinerie (f) *garden center*

jaune (m/f) *yellow*
jazz (m) *jazz*
je *I;* **je suis** *I am;* **je voudrais** *I would like*
jeans (m pl) *jeans*
jeu (m) *game:* **jeux vidéos** (m pl) *video games*
jeu de cartes (m) *pack of cards*
jeudi *Thursday*
jeune (m/f) *young*
joli(e) (adj: place, etc.) *nice; pretty*
jouer (verb) *to play*
jouet (m) *toy*
jour (m) *day*
journal (m) *newspaper*
joyeux anniversaire! *happy birthday!*
juillet *July*
juin *June*
jupe (f) *skirt*
jupon (m) *slip*
jus (m) *juice:* **jus d'orange** *orange juice;* **jus de fruit** (m) *fruit juice*
jusqu'à *until*
juste (adj) *right; fair* (correct); **ce n'est pas juste** *it's not fair*
juste un peu *just a little*

K, L

kilo (m) *kilo*
kilomètre (m) *kilometer*
klaxon (m) *horn* (car)
la *the* (f)
là *there;* **il n'est pas là** *he's out*
là-bas *over there*
lac (m) *lake*
lacet (m) *shoelace*
laid(e) (adj) *ugly*
laine (f) *wool*
laisse (f) *lead*
lait (m) *milk*
laitue (f) *lettuce*
lames de rasoir (f pl) *razor blades*
lampe (f) *lamp;* **lampe de bureau** *reading lamp;* **lampe de chevet** *bedside lamp;* **lampe de poche** (f) *torch*
landau (m) *pram*
langouste (f) *crayfish* (saltwater)
langue (f) *language; tongue*
lapin (m) *rabbit*
laque (f) *hairspray*
large (adj) *wide*
lavabo (m) *basin* (sink)
laverie automatique (f) *laundromat*

lave-vaisselle (m) *dishwasher*
laxatif (m) *laxative*
le *the* (m)
leçon (f) *lesson*
lecteur de cassettes (m) *cassette player*
léger, (fem) **légère** (adj) *light (not heavy)*
légumes (m pl) *vegetables*
lent(e) (adj) *slow*
lentilles *lenses* (f pl)
lentilles de contact (f pl) *contact lenses*
lentilles rigides *hard lenses;* **lentilles semi-souples** *gas-permeable lenses;* **lentilles souples** *soft lenses*
lequel, (fem) **laquelle: lequel?** *which?;* **n'importe lequel** *either of them*
les *the* (plural)
lessive (f) *powdered detergent*
lettre (f) *letter*
leur: leur chambre *their room;* **leurs livres** *their books*
levée (f) *postal collection*
lever: se lever (verb) *to get up*
levier de vitesse (m) *gearstick*
librairie (f) *bookshop*
libre (adj) *free* (at liberty)
lime à ongles (f) *nail file*
limitation de vitesse (f) *speed limit*
limonade (f) *lemonade*
linge (m) *laundry* (clothes)
lingettes (f pl) *baby wipes*
liqueur (f) *liqueur*
liquide *cash;* **payer en liquide** *to pay cash*
lire (verb) *to read*
liste (f) *list*
lit (m) *bed;* **lit d'enfant** (m) *cot*
litérature (f) *literature*
litre (m) *liter*
livraison (f) *delivery*
livre (m) *book; pound* (money, weight)
loin *far*
long, (fem) **longue** (adj) *long*
longueur (f) *length*
lotion solaire (f) *suntan lotion*
louer (verb) *to rent*
lourd(e) (adj) *heavy*
luge (f) *sled*
lumière (f) *light*
lundi *Monday*
lune (f) *moon;* **lune de miel** *honeymoon*

lunettes (f pl) *glasses, spectacles;* **lunettes de soleil** *sunglasses*
Luxembourg (m) *Luxembourg*

M

ma: ma maison *my house*
machine à laver (f) *washing machine*
maçon(ne) *bricklayer*
madame *madam;* **Madame** *Mrs.;* **madame!** *waitress!*
magasin (m) *shop;* **magasin d'antiquités** *antiques shop;* **magasin de disques** *record shop*
magnétoscope (m) *VCR*
mai *May*
maigre (m/f) (adj) *thin*
maillot de bain (m) *swimsuit; swimming trunks*
main (f) *hand*
maintenant *now*
mairie (f) *town hall*
mais *but*
maison (f) *house*
maître(resse) de conférences *university lecturer*
malade (adj) *ill*
mal à estomac (m) *stomachache*
mal à la tête (m) *headache*
mal de dents (m) *toothache*
mal de ventre (m) *stomachache*
manche (f) *sleeve*
Manche: la Manche *Channel*
mandarine (f) *tangerine*
manger (verb) *to eat*
manteau (m) *coat*
maquillage (m) *makeup*
marché (m) *market;* **marché couvert** (m) *indoor market*
marcher (verb) *to walk*
mardi *Tuesday*
marée (f) *tide*
margarine (f) *margarine*
mari (m) *husband*
mariage (m) *wedding*
marié(e) (adj) *married*
marmelade d'oranges (f) *marmalade*
marron (adj) *brown*
mars *March*
marteau (m) *hammer*
mascara (m) *mascara*
masque (m) *face mask*
mât (m) *mast*

match (m) *match* (sport)
matelas (m) *mattress;* **matelas pneumatique** *air mattress*
matin (m) *morning*
mauvais(e) (adj) *bad; poor* (bad quality); **mauvaises herbes** (f) *weeds*
mécanicien(ne) *mechanic*
médecin (m/f) *doctor*
médicaments (m pl) *medication*
médicine (m) *medicine* (subject)
Méditerranée: la Méditerranée (f) *Mediterranean*
méduse (f) *jellyfish*
meilleur: le/la meilleur(e) *the best*
melon (m) *melon*
même *same;* **le/la même...** *the same...;* **la même chose, s'il vous plaît** *the same again, please*
menu (m) *set menu*
mer (f) *sea*
merci *thank you*
mercredi *Wednesday*
mère (f) *mother*
mes: mes chaussures *my shoes*
message (m) *message*
messagerie (f): **messagerie électronique** *email;* **messagerie téléphonique** *voicemail*
messe (f) *mass* (church)
métro (m) *underground*
mettre (verb) *to put*
meublé(e) (adj) *furnished*
meubles (m pl) *furniture*
micro-ondes (m) *microwave*
midi (m) *noon*
miel (m) *honey*
mieux *better*
milieu (m) *middle*
mille *thousand*
mince (m/f) (adj) *thin*
minuit (m) *midnight*
minute (f) *minute*
miroir (m) *mirror*
mobylette (f) *moped*
mode (f) *fashion*
modem (m) *modem*
moi *me;* **c'est moi** *it's me;* **c'est pour moi;** *it's for me;* **c'est à moi** *it's mine*
moins *less*
mois (m) *month;* **les mois de l'année** *months of the year*
mon: mon livre *my book*
moniteur (m) *monitor* (computer)

monnaie (f) *change* (money)
monsieur *sir;* **Monsieur** *Mr.;* **monsieur!** *waiter!*
montagne (f) *mountain*
montant de tente (m) *tent pole*
monter (verb) *to get on* (bus etc)
montre (f) *watch*
monument (m) *monument*
morceau (m) *piece*
mordre (verb: by dog) *to bite*
morsure (f) *bite* (by dog)
mort(e) (adj) *dead*
mot (m) *word;* **mot de passe** (m) *password*
moteur (m) *engine* (car)
moto (f) *motorcycle*
mou, (fem) **molle** (adj) *soft*
mouche (f) *fly* (insect)
mouchoir (m) *handkerchief*
mouchoirs (m pl) *tissues*
mouillé(e) (adj) *wet*
moules (f pl) *mussels*
mourir (verb) *to die*
mousse (f) *mousse* (hair); **mousse à raser** (f) *shaving cream*
moustache (f) *moustache*
moustique (m) *mosquito*
moutarde (f) *mustard*
mur (m) *wall* (outside)
mûr(e) (adj) *ripe*
mûre (f) *blackberry*
musée (m) *museum;* **musée d'art** *art gallery*
musicien(ne) *musician;* **musicien(ne) des rues** *street musician*
musique (f) *music;* **musique classique** *classical music;* **musique folklorique** *folk music;* **musique forte** *loud music;* **musique pop** *pop music*

N

nager (verb) *to swim*
natation (f) *swimming*
navette (pour aéroport) (f) *airport bus*
né(e): je suis né(e) en... *I was born in...*
nécessaire *necessary;* **ce n'est pas nécessaire** *that's not necessary*
négatif (m) *negative* (photo)
négociant(e) en vins *wine merchant*
neige (f) *snow*

neuf *nine*
neuf, (fem) **neuve** *new*
neveu (m) *nephew*
nez (m) *nose*
ni: ni un ni autre *neither of them*; **ni… ni…** *neither… nor…*
nièce (f) *niece*
nier (verb) *to deny*
noir(e) *black*
noix (f) *nut* (fruit)
nom (m) *name*; **nom de famille** (m) *surname*
nombre (m) *number* (amount)
non *no*
nord (m) *north*
nos: nos enfants *our children*
notre: notre maison *our house*
nouer (verb) *to tie*
nourriture (f) *food*
nous *we*; **nous deux** *both of us*; **nous sommes** *we are*; **c'est à nous** *it's ours*; **c'est nous** *it's us*; **c'est pour nous** *it's for us*
nouveau, (fem) **nouvelle** *new*; **de nouveau** *again*
nouvelles (f pl) *news*
novembre *November*
nudiste (m/f) *nudist*
nuit (f) *night*
nulle part *nowhere*
numéro (m) *number* (figure)

O

objectif (m) *lens* (camera)
objets trouvés (m pl) *lost property*
obturateur (m) *shutter* (camera)
occupé(e) *busy* (occupied)
octobre *October*
odeur (f) *smell*
œil (m) *eye*
œuf (m) *egg*
office de tourisme (m) *tourist office*
oignon (m) *onion*
oiseau (m) *bird*
olive (f) *olive*
omelette (f) *omelet*
oncle (m) *uncle*
ondulé(e) (adj: hair) *wavy*
ongle (m) *nail* (finger)
onze *eleven*
opérateur(trice) *operator* (phone)
opération (f) *operation*
opticien(ne) *optician's*
or (m) *gold*
orage (m) *thunderstorm*
orange (f) *orange* (fruit, color)

orchestre (m) *orchestra; stalls* (theatre)
ordinateur (m) *computer;* **ordinateur portable** (m) *laptop*
ordonnance (f) *prescription*
ordre du jour (m) *agenda*
ordures (f pl) *litter; rubbish*
oreille (f) *ear*
oreiller (m) *pillow*
orgue (m) *organ* (music)
os (m) *bone*
ou *or*
où? *where?*
oublier (verb) *to forget*
ouest *west*
oui *yes*
ouvert(e) (adj) *open*
ouvre-boîte (m) *can opener*
ouvrir *to open*

P

page (f) *page*
paiement (m) *payment*; **paiement sans contact** *contactless payment*
pain (m) *bread*; **pain grillé** (m) *toast*
paire (f) *pair*
palais (m) *palace*
pâle (adj) *pale*
palmes (f pl) *flippers*
panier (m) *basket*
panne (f) *breakdown* (car); **je suis tombé(e) en panne** *I've had a breakdown*
pansement (m) *plaster*
pantalon (m) *trousers*
pantoufles (f pl) *slippers*
papa *dad*
papier (m) *paper*; **papier à lettres** *writing paper*; **papier cadeau** *gift wrap*; **papier d'emballage** *wrapping paper*; **papier filtre** *filter paper*; **papier hygiénique** *toilet paper*
paquet (m) *package, packet*
par: par avion *airmail*; **par chemin de fer** *by rail*; **par exemple** *for example*; **par nuit** *per night*
parapluie (m) *umbrella*
parasol (m) *sunshade*
parce que *because*
parcours de golf (m) *golf course*
pardon!, pardon? *excuse me!; sorry!* (apology); *pardon?*
pare-brise (m) *windscreen*
pare-chocs (m) *bumper*
parents (m pl) *parents*

paresseux(euse) (adj) *lazy*
parfait(e) (adj) *perfect*
parfum (m) *perfume*
parking (m) *parking lot*
parler (verb) *to speak, talk*; **parlez-vous…?** *do you speak…?*; **je ne parle pas…** *I don't speak…*
paroi (f) *wall* (inside)
parterre de fleurs (m) *flowerbed*
parti (m) *party* (political)
particulièrement *especially*
partout *everywhere*
pas *not*; **pas beaucoup** *not many*; **pas encore** *not yet*; **il n'est pas…** *he's not…*
passage (m) *crossing*
passager(ère) *passenger*
passeport (m) *passport*; **passeport pour animaux** (m) *pet passport*
passe-temps (m) *hobby*
pastilles pour la gorge (f pl) *throat lozenges*
pâtes (f pl) *pasta*
patinoire (f) *ice rink*
patins à glace (m pl) *ice skates*
pâtisserie (f) *cake shop*
pauvre (m/f) (also adj) *poor* (not rich)
payer (verb) *to pay*
pays (m) *country* (state); **pays de Galles** (m) *Wales*
pêche (f) *peach; fishing:* **aller à la pêche** (verb) *to go fishing*
peigne (m) *comb*
peigner *to comb*
peinture (f) *paint; painting*
pelle (f) *spade* (shovel)
pellicule couleur (f) *color film*
pelouse (f) *lawn*
pendant *during*
pendule (f) *clock*
penser (verb) *to think*
pension complète (f) *full board*
père (m) *father*
perle (f) *pearl*
permanente (f) *perm*
permis (m) *license*; **permis de conduire** (m) *driver's license*
personne *nobody*
personnel de chambre (m) *housekeeping* (at a hotel)
petit(e) (adj) *small*
petit ami (m) *boyfriend*
petit déjeuner (m) *breakfast*
petite amie (f) *girlfriend*
petite-fille (f) *granddaughter*

petit-fils (m) *grandson*
petits pois (m pl) *peas*
pétrole (m) *paraffin*
peut-être *maybe; perhaps*
phares (m pl) *headlights*
pharmacie (f) *chemist's*
photo (f) *photograph*
photographe (m/f) *photographer*
photographier to *photograph*
piano (m) *piano*
pickpocket (m/f) *pickpocket*
pièce (f) *coin; play* (theater)
pièce d'identité (f) *identification*
pièces de rechange (f pl) *spare parts*
pied (m) *foot*
piéton (m) *pedestrian*
pile (f) *battery* (torch)
pilote (m/f) *pilot*
pince (f): **pince à épiler** *tweezers;* **pince à linge** *peg;* **pince à ongles** *nail clippers*
pinceau (m) *paintbrush*
pipe (f) *pipe* (for smoking)
pique (m) *spades* (cards)
pique-nique (m) *picnic*
piquer (verb: by snake) *to bite;* (verb: by insect) *to sting*
piquet de tente (m) *tent peg*
piqûre (f) *bite* (by snake); *sting* (by insect); *injection*
pire *worse, worst*
piscine (f) *swimming pool*
piste (f) *runway; ski slope;* **piste pour débutants** *beginners' slope*
pistolet (m) *pistol*
piston (m) *piston*
pizza (f) *pizza*
placard (m) *cabinet*
place (f) *room* (space); *seat; square* (in town)
plafond (m) *ceiling*
plage(f) *beach*
plaisanterie (f) *joke*
plan (m) *town map*
plancher (m) *floor* (ground)
plan de travail (m) *worktop*
plancher (m) *floor* (ground)
plante (f) *plant*
plaque d'immatriculation (f) *license plate*
plastique (m) *plastic*
plat(e) (adj) *flat* (level)
plateau (m) *tray*

plats (m pl) *main courses;* **plats préparés** (m pl) *ready meals*
pleurer (verb) *to cry* (weep)
plombage (m) *filling* (in tooth)
plombier(ière) *plumber*
plongeoir (m) *diving board*
plonger (verb) *to dive*
pluie (f) *rain*
plus *more:* **plus de** *more than;* **plus tard** *later;* **plus ou moins** *more or less*
plusieurs *several*
plutôt *quite*
pneu (m) *tire;* **pneu crevé** (m) *flat tire*
poche (f) *pocket*
poêle (f) *frying pan*
poignée (f) *handle* (door)
poignet (m) *wrist*
poire (f) *pear*
poireau (m) *leek*
poison (m) *poison*
poisson (m) *fish*
poissonnerie (f)*fishmonger's*
poitrine (f) *chest*
poivre (m) *pepper* (and salt)
poivron (m) *bell pepper* (red/green)
police (f) *police*
policier(ière) (f) *police officer*
politique (f) *politics*
pommade (f) *ointment*
pomme (f) *apple*
pomme de terre (f) *potato*
pont (m) *bridge*
porc (m) *pork*
porcelaine (f) *china*
port (m) *harbor; port*
porte (f) *door* (building); **porte d'embarquement** (f) *gate* (at airport)
porte-bagages (m) *luggage rack*
portefeuille (m) *wallet*
porte-monnaie (m) *purse*
porteur(euse) *porter*
portière (f) *car door*
porto (m) *port* (drink)
possible *possible;* **dès que possible** *as soon as possible*
poste (f) *post; post office*
poster (m) *poster* (inside); (verb) *to post*
pot d'echappement (m) *exhaust* (car)
poubelle (f) *trash can*
poudre (f) *powder*
poulet (m) *chicken*
poupée (f) *doll*
pour *for;* **pour moi** *for me;* **pour une semaine** *for a week*

pourboire (m) *tip* (money)
pourquoi? *why?*
pousser (verb) *to push*
poussette (f) *stroller*
pouvoir (verb) *to be able;* **je peux avoir…?** *can I have…?;* **vous pouvez…?** *can you…?*
préférer (verb) *to prefer*
premier(ière) *first;* **premier étage** (m) *first floor;* **première classe** *first class;* **premiers soins** (m pl) *first aid*
prendre (verb) *to take;* **prendre le train** *take the train;* **prendre un bain** *have a bath*
prénom (m) *first name*
près de *near;* **près de la porte** *near the door;* **près de la fenêtre** *by the window*
préservatif (m) *condom*
presque *almost*
pressé(e): je suis pressé(e) *I'm in a hurry*
pressing (m) *dry cleaner's*
prêt(e) (adj) *ready*
prêtre (m) *priest*
prie: je vous en prie *you're welcome*
printemps (m) *spring* (season)
prise (f) *plug* (electrical); *electric car charger;* **prise multiple** *adaptor*
privé(e) (adj) *private*
prix (m) *price;* **prix d'entrée** *admission charge;* **prix du billet** (m) *fare*
problème (m) *problem;* **problème cardiaque** (m) *heart condition*
prochain(e) *next;* **la semaine prochaine** *next week*
produit pour la vaisselle (m) *dish soap*
produits de beauté (m pl) *cosmetics*
produits d'entretien (m pl) *household products*
produits laitiers (m pl) *dairy products*
produits surgelés (m pl) *frozen foods*
professeur(e) *professor; teacher* (secondary)
profession (f) *profession*
profond(e) *deep*
promener: aller se promener (verb) *to go for a walk*
propre (m/f) (adj) *clean*

prudent(e) (adj) *careful;*
  soyez prudent!
  be careful!
public (m) *public*
puce (f) *flea*
pull (m) *sweater*
punaise (f) *drawing pin*
pyjama (m) *pajamas*

Q

quai (m) *dock; platform*
qualité (f) *quality*
quand? *when?*
quarante *forty*
quart (m) *quarter*
quatorze *fourteen*
quatre *four*
quatre-vingt *eighty*
quatre-vingt-dix *ninety*
quatrième *fourth*
que *than*
quel âge avez-vous?
  how old are you?
quelle heure est-il? *what's
  the time?*
quelque chose *something*
quelque part *somewhere*
quelquefois *sometimes*
quelqu'un *somebody*
quelqu'un d'autre *someone
  else*
qu'est-ce que c'est? *what's
  that?; what is it?*
question (f) *question*
queue (f) *queue*
qui? *who?*
quincaillerie (f) *hardware
  shop*
quinze *fifteen;* **quinze jours**
  fortnight

R

radiateur (m) *heater; radiator*
radio (f) *x-ray; radio;* **service
  de radiologie** (m) *x-ray
  department*
radis (m) *radish*
rafraîchissements
  (m pl) *refreshments*
raie (f) *parting* (in hair)
raisin (m) *grape;* **raisin sec**
  (m) *raisin*
rallonge (f) *extension lead*
ramer (verb) *to row*
rames (f pl) *oars*
randonnée (f) *hiking*
rapide (m/f) (adj) *fast; quick*
rapport de police (m) *police
  report*
rare (m/f) *rare* (uncommon)
raser: se raser (verb) *to shave*
rat (m) *rat*

râteau (m) *rake*
rayon (m) *aisle*
  (supermarket)
réception (f) *reception*
receptionniste (m/f)
  receptionist
réclamation de bagages (f)
  baggage claim
**recommandé(e): en
  recommandé(e)** *registered
  post*
record (m) *record*
  (sports, etc.)
reçu (m) *receipt*
réduction (f) *discount*
**regarde: cela ne vous
  regarde pas** *it's none of
  your business*
regarder (verb) *to watch*
règle (f) *ruler*
rein (m) *kidney*
religion (f) *religion*
remercier (verb) *to thank*
remonte-pente (m)
  ski lift
remorque (f) *trailer*
rendez-vous (m)
  appointment
rendre (verb) *to return* (give
  back); **rendre visite** (verb:
  person) *visit*
repas (m) *meal*
repasser (verb) *to iron*
répondeur (m) *answering
  machine*
reposer: se reposer (verb)
  to rest (relax)
renseignements (m pl)
  directory (telephone)
réservation (f) *reservation*
réserver (verb) *to book,
  reserve*
résistant(e) (adj) *strong*
  (material)
respirer (verb) *to breathe*
ressort (m) *spring*
  (mechanical)
restaurant (m) *restaurant*
reste (m) *rest* (remainder)
retard (m) *delay*
retirer (verb) *to withdraw*
rétroviseur (m) *car mirror*
réunion (f) *meeting*
réveil (m) *alarm clock*
revenir (verb) *to return*
  (come back)
revue (f) *magazine*
rez-de-chaussée (m)
  ground floor
rhum (m) *rum*
rhume (m) *cold* (illness);
  rhume des foins (m)
  hay fever
riche (m/f) (adj) *rich*

rideau (m) *curtain*
rien *nothing;* **ça ne fait rien**
  it doesn't matter
rire (verb) *to laugh*
rivière (f) *river*
riz (m) *rice*
robe (f) *dress*
robinet (m) *tap* (water)
rocher (m) *rock* (stone)
rock (m) *rock* (music)
roman (m) *novel*
rond(e) (adj) *round* (circular)
rondelle (f) *washer*
rond-point (m)
  roundabout
room service (m) *room
  service*
rose (f) *rose;* (adj) *pink*
rôti(e) (adj) *roasted*
roue (f) *wheel*
rouge *red;* **rouge à lèvres**
  (m) *lipstick*
rougeur (f) *rash*
rouleaux (m pl) *curlers*
roux *red* (of hair)
rue (f) *street*
rugby (m) *rugby*
ruines (f pl) *ruins*
ruisseau (m) *stream* (small
  river)

S

sa: sa maison *his/her house*
sable (m) *sand*
sac (m) *bag;* **sac à dos**
  backpack; **sac à main**
  handbag; **sac de
  couchage** *sleeping bag;*
  sac poubelle *trash can
  liner*
saignant *rare* (steak)
salade (f) *salad*
salle (f) *room;* **salle à
  manger** *dining room;*
  salle d'attente
  waiting room;
  salle d'opérations
  operating room;
  salle de bains *bathroom;*
  salle de conférences
  conference room
salon (m) *living room*
salut *hi*
samedi *Saturday*
sandales (f pl) *sandals*
sandwich (m) *sandwich*
sang (m) *blood*
sans *without;* **sans plomb**
  unleaded
santé! *cheers!*
s'arrêter (verb) *to stop*
sauce (f) *sauce*
saucisse (f) *sausage*

saumon (m) *salmon*
sauna (m) *sauna*
savoir (verb) *to know* (fact);
 je ne sais pas *I don't know*
savon (m) *soap*
science (f) *science*
seau (m) *bucket*
sec, (fem) sèche (adj) *dry*
sèche-cheveux (m)
 hair dryer
seconde (f) *second*
 (of time)
seconde: en seconde
 second class
secrétaire (m/f) *secretary*
sécurité: en sécurité *safe*
 (*not in danger*)
seize *sixteen*
sel (m) *salt*
semaine (f) *week*
séminaire (m) *seminar*
sentir (verb) *to smell*
séparé(e) (adj) *separate*
séparer (verb) *to separate*
sept *seven*
septembre *September*
sérieux(euse) (adj) *serious*
seringue (f) *syringe*
séropositif(ve) *HIV positive*
serveur (m) *waiter*
serveuse (f) *waitress*
service de pédiatrie (m)
 children's ward
serviette (f) *towel*
serviettes hygiéniques
 (f pl) *sanitary napkins*
ses: ses chaussures *his/her
 shoes*
seul(e) *alone; single* (one)
seulement *only*
shampooing (m) *shampoo*
short (m) *shorts*
si *if; whether*
SIDA *AIDS*
siège pour bébé (m) *car seat*
 (*for a baby*)
siège social (m) *head office*
silencieux(euse) (adj) *quiet*
 (person)
s'il vous plaît *please*
simple (adj) *simple*
sirop (m) *syrup*
site web (m) *website*
six *six*
ski (m) *ski;* **faire du ski**
 to go skiing
skier (verb) *to ski*
slip (m) *underpants*
snack (m) *snack*
sœur(f) *sister*
soie (f) *silk*
soif: j'ai soif *I'm thirsty*
soir (m) *evening;* **ce soir**
 tonight

soirée (f) *party* (get together)
soit… soit… *either… or…*
soixante *sixty*
soixante-dix *seventy*
soldes (f pl) *sale* (at reduced
 prices)
soleil (m) *sun*
solution de trempage (f)
 contact solution
 (*for contact lenses*)
sommeil (m) *sleep*
somnifère (m) *sleeping pill*
son livre *his/her book*
sonnette (f) *bell* (door)
sortie (f) *exit*
sortie de secours (f)
 emergency exit
sortir (verb) *to leave*
soucoupe (f) *saucer*
soûl(e) (adj) *drunk*
soupape (f) *valve*
soupe (f) *soup*
souper (m) *supper*
sourcil (m) *eyebrow*
sourd(e) (adj) *deaf*
sourire (m) *smile;* (verb)
 to smile
souris (f) *mouse*
sous… *below…; under…*
sous-sol (m) *basement*
sous-vêtement (m)
 underwear
soutien-gorge (m) *bra*
souvenir (m) *souvenir;* (verb)
 remember; **je m'en
 souviens** *I remember;*
 je ne me souviens pas
 I don't remember
souvent *often*
sport(m) *sport*
stade (m) *stadium*
stagiaire (m) *trainee*
station (f) *underground
 station*
station de ski (f) *ski resort*
station-service (f) *gas station*
statue (f) *statue*
steak (m) *steak*
store (m) *blind* (window)
stupide (adj) *stupid*
stylo (m) *pen;* **stylo-bille**
 (m) *ballpoint pen;* **stylo
 plume** (m) *fountain pen*
sucette (f) *lollipop*
sucre (m) *sugar*
sucré(e) (adj) *sweet*
 (not sour)
sud (m) *south*
suisse (adj) *Swiss* (m/f)
Suisse: la Suisse
 Switzerland
supermarché (m)
 supermarket
supplément (m) *supplement*

suppositoire (m) *suppository*
sur… *on…*
sûr(e) *sure*
survêtement (m) *tracksuit*
sweat-shirt (m) *sweatshirt*
sympathique (adj: person)
 nice
synagogue (f) *synagogue*

T

ta: ta maison *your house*
 (singular informal)
tabac (m) *tobacco;
 tobaconnist/newsagent's*
table (f) *table*
tablette de chocolat (f) *bar
 of chocolate*
taille (f) *size*
taille-crayon (m) *pencil
 sharpener*
talc (m) *talcum powder*
talon (m) *heel*
tampon (m) *tampon*
tante (f) *aunt*
tapis (m) *carpet, rug* (mat);
 tapis de sol (m)
 groundsheet
tapisserie (f) *tapestry*
tard late; bus est en retard
 the bus is late
tasse (f) *cup; mug*
taux de change (m)
 exchange rate
taxi (m) *taxi*
tee-shirt (m) *T-shirt*
téléphérique (m) *cable car*
téléphone (m) *telephone;*
 téléphone portable (m)
 mobile phone
téléphoner (verb)
 to telephone
télévision (f) *television*
télévision par câble (f)
 cable TV
témoin (m/f) *witness*
température (f) *temperature*
tempête (f) *storm;*
 tempête de neige (f)
 blizzard
temps (m) *weather; time;*
 de temps en temps
 occasionally
tennis (m) *tennis;*
 les tennis (f pl) *sneakers*
tente (f) *tent*
terminal (m) *terminal*
terrain de camping (m)
 campsite
terrasse (f) *terrace*
terre (f) *land; soil*
tes: tes chaussures
 your shoes (singular
 informal; plural noun)

tête (f) *head*
thé (m) *tea*
théâtre (m) *theater*
ticket (m) *ticket* (underground, bus)
timbre (m) *stamp*
tire-bouchon (m) *corkscrew*
tirer (verb) *to pull*
tiroir (m) *drawer*
tissu (m) *material*
toboggan (m) *toboggan*
toi: c'est à toi *it's yours*
toilettes (f pl) *toilets*
toit (m) *roof*
tomate (f) *tomato*
ton: ton livre *your book* (singular informal)
tondeuse à gazon (f) *lawn mower*
tongs (f pl) *flip-flops*
tonic (m) *tonic*
torchon (m) *dish cloth*
tôt *early*
toucher (verb) *to feel, touch*
toujours *always*
tour (f) *tower*
tourisme (m) *sightseeing*
touriste (m/f) *tourist*
tourne-disque (m) *record player*
tournevis (m) *screwdriver*
tous les deux *both of them*
tousser (verb) *to cough*
tout *all; everything;*
   tout droit *straight on;* **tout le monde** *everyone;* **tout seul** *all alone*
toux (f) *cough*
tracteur (m) *tractor*
tradition (f) *tradition*
traducteur(trice) *translator*
traduire (verb) *to translate*
train (m) *train*
tranquille (adj: street, etc.) *quiet*
transpiration (f) *sweat*
transpirer (verb) *to sweat*
travail (m) *job; work*
travailler (verb: person) *to work*
traverser (verb) *to cross over*
trèfle (m) *clubs* (cards)
treize *thirteen*
trente *thirty*
très *very*
tricoter *knit*
triste (adj) *sad*
trois *three*
troisième *third*
tromper: se tromper (verb) *to be mistaken*
trop *too* (excessively)

trottoir (m) *pavement*
tu *you* (singular informal);
   tu es *you are*
tunnel (m) *tunnel;* **le tunnel sous La Manche** *Channel Tunnel*
tuyau (m) *pipe, hose* (for water)

U

un/une *a; one;*
   un/une autre *another* (different)
université (f) *university*
urgence (f) *emergency;*
   service des urgences (m) *emergency department*
urgent(e) (adj) *urgent*
utensiles de cuisine (f pl) *cooking utensils*
utile (adj) *useful*
utiliser (verb) *to use*

V

vacances (f pl) *holiday*
vaccin (m) *vaccine*
vaccination (f) *vaccination*
vacciner (verb) *to vaccinate*
vague (f) *wave;* (adj) *faint*
valise (f) *case*
valise (f) *suitcase*
vallée (f) *valley*
vanille (f) *vanilla*
vapeur: à la vapeur (adj) *steamed*
vase (m) *vase*
veau (m) *veal*
végétarien(ne) (adj) *vegetarian*
véhicule (m) *vehicle*
vélo (m) *bicycle;* **vélo tout terrain** (m) *mountain bike*
vendre (verb) *to sell*
vendredi *Friday*
venir (verb) *to come;*
   je viens de… *I come from…*
vent (m) *wind*
vente (f) *sale* (transaction)
ventilateur (m) *fan* (ventilator)
vernis à ongles (m) *nail polish*
verre (m) *glass*
verrou (m) *bolt* (on door)
verrouiller (verb) *to bolt*
vert(e) *green*
veste (f) *jacket*
vêtements (m pl) *clothes*
vétérinaire (m/f) *vet*
viande (f) *meat*

vide (adj) *empty*
vidéo (f) *video (film/tape)*
vie (f) *life*
vieux, (fem) vieille (adj) *old*
villa (f) *villa*
village (m) *village*
ville (f) *city; town*
vin (m) *wine*
vinaigre (m) *vinegar*
vingt *twenty*
violet(te) *purple*
violon (m) *violin*
vis (f) *screw*
visage (m) *face*
viseur (m) *viewfinder*
visite (f) *tour; visit*
visiter (verb) *to visit* (place)
visiteur(euse) *visitor*
vitesse (f) *gear* (car); *speed*
vodka (f) *vodka*
voile (f) *sailing*
voilier (m) *sailing boat*
voir (verb) *to see;* **je vois** *I see;* **je ne vois rien** *I can't see anything*
voiture (f) *car; train carriage*
voix (f) *voice*
vol (m) *flight*
volaille (f) *poultry*
volant (m) *steering wheel*
voler (verb) *to fly; steal;* **on a volé(e)** *it's been stolen*
volet (m) *shutter* (window)
voleur(euse) *thief*
vomir (verb) *to be sick* (vomit)
vos: vos chaussures *your shoes* (singular formal; plural; plural noun)
votre: votre maison *your house* (singular formal; plural; singular noun)
vouloir (verb) *to want;* **je veux** *I want;* **vous voulez?** *do you want?*
vous *you* (singular formal; plural); **vous êtes** *you are*
voyage (m) *journey*
vrai(e) *true*
vue (f) *view*

W, Y, Z

wagon-lit (m) *sleeping car*
wagon-restaurant (m) *restaurant car*
whisky (m) *whisky*
yaourt (m) *yogurt*
yeux (m pl) *eyes*
zoo (m) *zoo*

Acknowledgments

FOURTH EDITION (2023)

For this edition, the publisher would like to thank Nandini D Tripathy for editorial assistance; Ira Sharma for design assistance; Nityanand Kumar for DTP assistance; Sara Sanchez and Bethan Renwick for the editorial review; Karen Constanti for assistance with artwork commissioning; Peter Bull Art Studio and Dan Crisp for illustrations; and Andiamo! Language Services Ltd for foreign language proofreading.

THIRD EDITION (2018)
Senior Editors Angeles Gavira, Christine Stroyan
Project Art Editor Vanessa Marr
DTP Designer John Goldsmid
Jacket Design Development Manager Sophia MTT
Jacket Designer Juhi Sheth
Pre-Producer David Almond
Senior Producer Ana Vallarino
Associate Publisher Liz Wheeler
Publishing Director Jonathan Metcalf

FIRST EDITION (2005)
The publisher would like to thank the following for their help in the preparation of this book: Anne-Marie Miller for the organization of location photography in France; Hôtel-Restaurant, "Le Rabelais," Fontenay le Comte; Gare Routière de Fontenay le Comte; Pharmacie Parot, Nieul Sur L'Autise; Garage Gouband, Oulmes; Musée de l'Abbaye de Nieul Sur L'Autise (Cabinet Tetrac, Nantes); Boulangerie des familles, Coulon; Fromagerie, rue St. Marthe, Niort; Fruits et Primeurs Benoit, Halles de Niort; Gare SNCF de Niort; Magnet Showroom, Enfield, MyHotel, London; Kathy Gammon; Juliette Meeus, and Harry.

Produced for Dorling Kindersley by Schermuly Design Co.
Language content for Dorling Kindersley by g-and-w publishing
Managed by Jane Wightwick
Editing and additional input Pamela Wightwick, Christine Arthur, Leila Gaafar
Additional design assistance Phil Gamble, Lee Riches, Fehmi Cömert, Sally Geeve
Additional editorial assistance Kajal Mistry, Paul Docherty, Lynn Bresler
Picture research Louise Thomas

PICTURE CREDITS

The publisher would like to thank the following for their kind permission to reproduce their photographs.

Key: a-above; b-below/bottom; c-centre; f-far; l-left; r-right; t-top

2 Dreamstime.com: Beatrice Preve (tc). **Getty Images / iStock:** csfotoimages (bc). **3 DK Images:** Peter Wilson (tl), (bl); **Dreamstime.com:** Bo Li (tr). **Shutterstock.com:** Weho (br). **4-5 Alamy:** f1 Online tl; images-of-france (tr). **Alamy:** Andy Marshall (bl); **DK Images:** (br); Neil Lukas (tcr). **6-7 Laura Knox:** (cl). **9 Getty Images:** Maskot (cla). **10 Getty Images / iStock:** Morsa Images / E+ (cb). **11 Getty Images / iStock:** pixdeluxe (cl). **12 Getty Images / iStock:** stocknroll (cr). **13 Dreamstime.com:** Monkey Business Images (br). **Getty Images / iStock:** kali9 / E+ (cla); monkeybusinessimages (cl). **14 Dreamstime.com:** Nyul (crb/ old woman). **Getty Images / iStock:** Prostock-Studio (crb). **15 Dreamstime.com:** Slobodan Mra˘cina (cr); Arne9001 (cla); Pressmaster (tl); **Ingram Image Library:** (cBl), (cAr); **Getty Images / iStock:** agrobacter (cl). **17 Getty Images / iStock:** Morsa Images / E+ (bl); pixdeluxe (cl). **19 Alamy Stock Photo:** nito (cb). **21 Getty Images:** 10'000 Hours / DigitalVision (cla). **23 DK Images:** Dave King (tcl). **24 Getty Images:** Stuart Snelling / EyeEm (cr). **25 Dorling Kindersley:** Maison and Jardin, Orlando, Florida (cla). **Getty Images / iStock:** monkeybusinessimages (clb, bl); ShotShare (cl). **26 Dreamstime.com:** Monkey Business Images (cr). **Getty Images / iStock:** kuppa_rock (tr). **28 Dreamstime.com:** Robert Kneschke (br). **29 Alamy Stock Photo:** PhotoAlto (bl). **Shutterstock.com:** Africa Studio (clb); by-studio (cl). **30 DK Images:** (cr), (bcr). **31 Getty Images / iStock:** AsiaVision / E+ (cl). **32 Getty Images / iStock:** kupicoo / E+ (cr). **33 Getty Images / iStock:** Moon Safari (cla, cl, clb).

34-35 Dreamstime.com: Jiri Hera (ca). **34 Dreamstime.com:** Roman Egorov (c). **Getty Images:** Halfdark / fStop (crb). **Shutterstock.com:** Araddara (cb). **35 Dreamstime.com:** Oleg Dudko (cl). **36 DK Images:** (br). **Dreamstime.com:** Oleg Dudko (ca/Cordless Phone); Roman Egorov (ca). **36-37 Dreamstime.com:** Jiri Hera (tc). **37 Getty Images:** Halfdark / fStop (cla); Stuart Snelling / EyeEm (bl). **38 Dreamstime.com:** Rosshelen (cr). **40 Dreamstime.com:** Leonid Andronov (bl).; **Alamy:** Justin Kase (cr). **41 Shutterstock.com:** Vereshchagin Dmitry (cl). **42 Dreamstime.com:** Jose Hernandez (cr). **43 Alamy Stock Photo:** Cultura Creative RF (tl); Cultura RM (cla); Andy Marshall (cl). **44 Shutterstock.com:** Nerthuz (c). **46 Dreamstime.com:** Leonid Andronov (cla). **Shutterstock.com:** Vereshchagin Dmitry (ca); Nerthuz (cr). **47 Dreamstime.com:** Rosshelen (bl). **48-49 Alamy Stock Photo:** Ian G Dagnall (cb); Peter Titmuss (bc). **49 Dreamstime.com:** Bo Li (bl). **Getty Images / iStock:** csfotoimages (tl). **50-51 Dreamstime.com:** Sergey Dzyuba (c). **52 Getty Images / iStock:** krblokhin (cr). **53 Alamy Stock Photo:** Hisham Ibrahim (cla/Restroom); imageBROKER (cla); Image Farm Inc. (cla/sign). **54 Alamy Stock Photo:** Moodboard Stock Photography (cr). **Getty Images / iStock:** martin-dm / E+ (crb). **55 Dreamstime.com:** Vinicius Tupinamba (cla). **Getty Images / iStock:** xavierarnau / E+ (tl); **DK Images:** Andy Crawford (bl). **56 Alamy Stock Photo:** Ian G Dagnall (cr); Pictures Colour Library (ca); Peter Titmuss (c). **Dreamstime.com:** Bo Li (ca/Museum). **Shutterstock.com:** Nerthuz (bc); Evgeny Shmulev (cl). **58 Dreamstime.com:** David Brooks (cr). **Getty Images / iStock:** zeljkosantrac / E+ (crb). **59 Alamy Stock Photo:** Michael Juno (cla). **Getty Images / iStock:** 0802290022 (clb). **60 Getty Images / iStock:** surachetsh (cb). **Shutterstock.com:** Sarymsakov Andrey (c). **61 Alamy Stock Photo:** Cultura Creative RF (cl). **Dreamstime.com:** Piotr Adamowicz (bl). **Getty Images / iStock:** yipengge (tl). **62-63 Dreamstime.com:** Jennifer Thompson (c). **64 Dreamstime.com:** Beatrice Preve (crb). **65 Alamy Stock Photo:** Arcaid Images (clb/Bathroom). **Dreamstime.com:** Apiwan Borrikonratchata (cla/car trunk); Vitalyedush (cla). **Getty Images / iStock:** piovesempre (clb/bedroom). **Shutterstock.com:** Sarymsakov Andrey (cl/Hotel Room). **66 Alamy Stock Photo:** Arcaid Images (c). **Dreamstime.com:** Jennifer Thompson (b). **68 Alamy Stock Photo:** doughoughton (cr); Justin Kase RF (bl); F1online digitale Bildagentur GmbH / Alex Bartel (crb). **Shutterstock.com:** Weho (cra). **69 Alamy Stock Photo:** Bartomeu Amengual (cl); ImagesEurope (clb). **Getty Images / iStock:** nastya_ph (tl); TkKurikawa (cla). **72 Alamy:** Image Source (cr); **Getty Images / iStock:** doomu (bl). **73 Dreamstime.com:** Charlieaja (tl). **74 Getty Images:** Alessandro Ventura / beyond fotomedia (cr). **76 Alamy Stock Photo:** Bartomeu Amengual (crb); F1online digitale Bildagentur GmbH / Alex Bartel (cb). **Getty Images / iStock:** PK-Photos (cr). **79 Getty Images / iStock:** shapecharge / E+ (tl, cla, cl, clb). **Shutterstock.com:** Zhu Difeng (bl). **80 Dreamstime.com:** Robert Kneschke (cra). **80-81 Getty:** Taxi / Rob Melnychuk (bc); **Ingram Image Library:** (tl). **81 Dreamstime.com:** Photographerlondon (bl). **82 Alamy Stock Photo:** JSP Studios / Momentum Creative (cr). **Getty Images / iStock:** Bim (crb). **Shutterstock.com:** Gorodenkoff (cra). **83 Alamy Stock Photo:** wildphotos.com (tl). **84-85 Shutterstock.com:** Pressmaster (c). **84 Shutterstock.com:** Ground Picture (bl). **85 Getty Images / iStock:** PeopleImages (ca). **Shutterstock.com:** Drazen Zigic (cb). **86-87 Getty:** Taxi / Rob Melnychuk (tc). **89 Dreamstime.com:** Sebnem Ragiboglu (cla). **91 Dorling Kindersley:** Stephen Oliver (cl). **Getty Images / iStock:** Damir Khabirov (tl). **92 Getty Images / iStock:** E+ / FatCamera (cr). **93 Dreamstime.com:** Roman Egorov (br); Prostockstudio (tl). **94 Getty Images / iStock:** E+ / Morsa Images (cra); E+ / Tempura (br). **95 DK Images:** Stephen Oliver (cla); **Dreamstime.com:** Shawn Hempel (clb/Vial). **Getty Images / iStock:** seb_ra (clb). **97 Dreamstime.com:** Prostockstudio (bc). **98 Dreamstime.com:** Rawf88 (bl). **98-99 Alamy Stock Photo:** Trevor Pearson (c). **99 Alamy Stock Photo:** Itsik Marom (ca). **Getty Images / iStock:** E+ / CreativaStudio (cr). **Shutterstock.com:** Gajus (tl). **100 Dreamstime.com:** Draftmode (cb). **Getty Images / iStock:** sihuo0860371 (cr). **102 Getty Images / iStock:** cjp (cra). **102-103 Getty Images / iStock:** DigiStu (b). **103 Dreamstime.com:** Welcomia (cla). **Getty Images / iStock:** Imagesines (tl). **104-105 DK Images:** Paul Bricknell (cl(6)); Jane Burton (bcl); Geoff Dann (cl(1)); Max Gibbs (cl(2)); Frank Greenaway (cl(3)); Dave King (cl(4)), (cAr); Tracy Morgan (cl(5)). **106-107 Getty Images / iStock:** sihuo0860371 (b). **106 Dreamstime.com:** Draftmode (bc). **107 Alamy Stock Photo:** Itsik Marom (cl). **Getty Images / iStock:** DigiStu (bc). **109 Getty Images / iStock:** mediaphotos (cla). **110 Getty Images / iStock:** Biserka Stojanovic (cr). **111 Dreamstime.com:** Welcomia (clb). **112 Getty Images / iStock:** E+ / freemixer (cr). **113 Dreamstime.com:** Antonio Guillem (tl). **Shutterstock.com:** Evgeny Atamanenko (clb). **114 Dreamstime.com:** Amsis1 (br); Brett Critchley (crb). **Getty Images / iStock:** Ridofranz (cr). **115 Alamy Stock Photo:** REUTERS / Christian Hartmann (br). **Dreamstime.com:** Ulianna19970 (tl). **Getty Images / iStock:** Tatsiana Volkava (cla). **116 Dreamstime.com:** Welcomia (cra). **Getty Images / iStock:** mediaphotos (br). **118-119 Dreamstime.com:** Vladwitty (c). **119 Dreamstime.com:** Prostockstudio (cr). **120 Dreamstime.com:** Sergeyoch (bc); Wavebreakmedia Ltd (cr); Volkop (bc/Racket). **121 Getty Images / iStock:** E+ / AscentXmedia (tl). **122-123 Alamy Stock Photo:** Tony Tallec (c). **123 Getty Images / iStock:** nastya_ph (cla). **124 Dreamstime.com:** Wavebreakmedia Ltd (bc); **DK Images:** Paul Bricknell (tc(2)); Geoff Dann (tc(5)); Max Gibbs (tc(3)); Frank Greenaway (tc(4)); Dave King (tc(1)); Tracy Morgan (tc(6)). **126 Alamy Stock Photo:** Trevor Pearson (c). **127 Alamy Stock Photo:** PhotoAlto (tc). **Shutterstock.com:** Africa Studio (ca); **Getty Images / iStock:** pixdeluxe (cr). **128 DK Images:** Neil Mersh.

All other images © Dorling Kindersley.